A scene from the Arizona Theatre Company production of "Dracula." Set design by

Photo by Tim Fuller

DRACULA

BY
STEVEN DIETZ

FROM THE NOVEL BY
BRAM STOKER

★

DRAMATISTS
PLAY SERVICE
INC.

DRACULA
Copyright © 1996, Steven Dietz

All Rights Reserved

SPECIAL NOTE

Originally produced by the
Arizona Theatre Company Tucson/Phoenix, Arizona.
David Ira Goldstein, Artistic Director
Robert Alpaugh, Managing Director

For David Ira Goldstein

and

Roberta Carlson

and

the Actors named herein ...

DRACULA was commissioned by, and received its premiere at, the Arizona Theatre Company (David Ira Goldstein, Artistic Director), in Tucson, Arizona, on March 31st, 1995. It was directed by David Ira Goldstein; the set design was by Bill Forrester; the costume design was by David Kay Mickelsen; the lighting design was by Don Darnutzer; the original music was by Roberta Carlson; the sound design was by Jeff Ladman; and the stage manager was George Darveris. The cast was as follows:

RENFIELD .... David Pichette
MINA .... Britt Sady
LUCY .... Suzanne Bouchard
HARKER .... David Ellenstein
SEWARD .... Benjamin Livingston
DRACULA .... Patrick Page
VAN HELSING .... Peter Silbert
WAITERS, VIXENS, ATTENDANTS, MAIDS .... Adam Burke,
            Jamie Lynn Hines, Aubdon O. Morales, Renee Serino

ACKNOWLEDGEMENT

The author wishes to thank David Ira, once again, for his faith in me; Steitzer and Pichette, who began my formal education in all things gothic and *vampiric;* and Allison, for listening well into the night ...

CHARACTERS
(5 men, 2 women)

MINA — a woman in her early twenties
HARKER — her fiancé, a solicitor
LUCY — Mina's friend
SEWARD — Lucy's suitor, head of a lunatic asylum
RENFIELD — a madman
VAN HELSING — a professor
DRACULA — a Count from Transylvania

Additional Actors (2 women, 1 man), who play:
WAITERS
ATTENDANTS
MAID
VIXENS

TIME and PLACE

1897.
London, England. And Transylvania.

SETTING

The play moves quickly amid numerous environments, the primary ones being: Lucy's bedroom, Renfield's cell, Dracula's castle, and the guest room at the asylum. A few specific pieces, generally called for within the scene, should suffice for each. Above all, nothing should hinder the constant, fluid motion from one scene to the next.

MUSIC

Two things. The ability to get under our skin, almost sublimi-nally, from time to time. And, of course, the ability to bom-bard us with terror, when needed. (The author highly recom-mends Roberta Carlson's original score, composed for the pre-miere production of this play at the Arizona Theatre Company, March 1995. For information on Ms. Carlson's music, please contact her at 214 Oak Grove, Minneapolis, MN 55403. Tele-phone: 612-874-0395.)

EFFECTS

This play was written to be produced in a variety of theaters — large and small; lavishly equipped or typically impoverished.

Blood should be plentiful.
A good sound system is necessary.

Beyond that, nearly ALL the effects called for in the text can be either *simplified* or, in some instances, *deleted*. Some alter-nate suggestions appear in the stage directions throughout. Others are, obviously, left to the discretion of the production. In the end, if the characters — and thus, the audience — take the power and terror of Dracula seriously, the effects (be they large or small) will simply lend credence to this terror. It's important, in fact, that no effect ever take us "out of the play," for, ultimately, the motion and clarity of the story is para-mount.

Don't believe for a moment that he is killing the young.
He is costuming angels.

—Jean Cocteau

DRACULA

ACT ONE

Music from the darkness. Lights rise on —

A small table, far downstage, in front of the curtain. The table is set, elegantly, for one. In the chair at the table sits a man wearing a black tuxedo. This is Renfield. He places his napkin on his lap. He snaps his fingers. A Waiter enters and fills the wine glass on the table. Red, of course. The Waiter goes. Renfield sips his wine. He looks out at the audience.

RENFIELD.
    We are all of us invented.
    We are all of us cobbled together from cartilage and dust.
    Few of us know with certainty the name of our maker.
    But, I do.
(He raises a picture that is face down on the table [or: a slide is projected onto the curtain.] It is a picture of:)

    Bram Stoker

Born eight November, eighteen forty-seven. Dublin. A sickly child who loved his mother. A young man who, like all young men, fell in with a crowd. Yes, *that* crowd. That *theatre* crowd. And our young Bram entered the theatrical profession in as low and base a manner as one possibly can.

As a critic. *(He snaps his fingers — the Waiter enters, carrying a covered silver platter. He/she places it in front of Renfield, but does not uncover it. Then, the Waiter exits.)* In 1897, at age fifty, Bram Stoker published a book that would, in time, become his definitive work. In doing so, he made *me*. And he gave to me a name: *Renfield*. And, he gave me something more. Something that so many of you wish for, pray for, beg for — and, yet, will never attain. *Immortality. (He smiles a bit. Sips his wine. His expression changes.)* I have never forgiven him that. *(Renfield lifts the cover of the platter, revealing — A large, brown rat ... still alive. Music. Sound of manic laughter and screaming. Renfield lifts the squirming rat by the tail and dangles it above his head, lowering it down into his mouth, as — Three Attendants, in white coats, rush on and grab Renfield. As he is yanked up out of his chair, he is also yanked out of his tuxedo, revealing his grey/green asylum clothing. This happens as — The curtain opens, and — Renfield is hauled away U. into the distance, laughing, screaming, the rat halfway in his mouth, as — music crescendos, then stops abruptly, as lights shift to — Lucy's Room. Sunset. A bed and a large window are prominent. Long, thick black drapes frame the window. Mina sits on the edge of the bed, holding a business notebook. Lucy sits in the middle of the bed, listening to Mina. Sound of a clock ticking.)*

MINA.   And that way, after we are married, I'll be able to serve as Jonathan's stenographer —

LUCY.   Mm hmm.

MINA.   I will write down his thoughts in shorthand —

LUCY.   Mm hmm.

MINA.   Then, later, transcribe them onto a typewriter — and therefore be of great help to him in his work as a solicitor.

LUCY.   How fascinating. *(Lucy gradually stands on the bed, behind Mina. Mina does not notice, referring still to her notebook.)*

MINA.   He is keeping a journal of his business trip abroad —

LUCY.   A journal? Really? *(Lucy has pulled a sheet up from the bed and is wearing it as a cape. Mina remains unaware.)*

MINA.   Yes, in shorthand. And, when he returns I shall put my new training to work.

LUCY.   I see. *(Lucy stands behind Mina, looking down at her threateningly.)*

MINA. I've been practicing very hard. Shorthand is a more difficult art than many people realize. It requires a — *(Lucy whips her "cape" over Mina, and pounces on her.)*
LUCY. Be mine be mine forever! *(Mina screams, then they both begin laughing and giggling as they roll around on the bed. Lucy is tickling Mina.)*
MINA. Lucy, stop it —
LUCY. I won't stop till you put an end to all this talk of shorthand and journals and business —
MINA. I haven't seen you in months. I thought you'd —
LUCY. So don't talk to me of numbers and letters. Tell me about your heart.
MINA. My heart is resolute.
LUCY. Forget your heart. Tell me of your body. Tell me what thoughts of Jonathan do to your skin and your blood and your bones —
MINA. Lucy, you're shameful —
LUCY. Then shame me. You're my one true girlfriend. You alone can talk to me of the things that dare not leave this room. *(Lucy touches Mina's face, tenderly.)* Please. *(Silence. Mina stares at her.)* Very well. You've become a practical young woman, about to marry a man who leaves you cold.
MINA. No. Not cold. *(Smiles a bit.)* Not cold at all. *(Lucy moves in closer to her.)* Sometimes I think of his touch and my hands tremble. My lips become wet. I can feel my heart beating in my throat.
LUCY. *(A devilish, delicious smile.)* Oh, Mina ...
MINA. He's only been gone a week, and already I ache for him. *(A shaft of light rises on Harker, wearing a coat. On the ground next to him are his valise, and briefcase. His spirit is buoyant. Faint sound of a bell tolling; trees rustling.)* When a letter arrives from him, his words make my hopes sing.
HARKER. My darling Mina, I write to you from the heart of the Carpathian Mountains. I am spending the night in Bistritz, at a fine hotel recommended by my client, the Count. Tomorrow, he'll send a carriage for and we'll begin our work at his castle. I'm told this region, known as Transylvania, is one of the wildest and least known portions of Europe. How

fortunate that my work allows me exotic trips to strange and distant countries. And the food! Tonight, I had an eggplant stuffed with forcemeat which they call "impletata." *(Smiles.)* Before you ask, the answer is "Yes" — I did get a copy of the recipe for you. After dinner, a strange old woman — reeking of garlic — took me aside and told me that tomorrow is St. George's Day, and I should not travel to visit the Count. She began wailing that at midnight the dead spirits will rise and evil will hold sway over the world. Such amusing pagans these people are! She went so far as to press her rosary into my hands — *(He holds up the rosary, with a large crucifix attached.)* — which I've kept as a souvenir of the delightful earnestness of these simple, misguided souls. Oh, my sweet Mina, how my heart rejoices at the thought of you. I'll be home safely and soon. Your loving husband-to-be ... Jonathan. *(Lights out on Harker, as — Lucy overlaps his last word, throwing herself at Mina, playfully —.)*

LUCY.   Jonathan! *(They wrestle about on the bed, laughing. Lucy cups her hand over Mina's mouth and kisses the back of it, pretending to be Harker.)* Oh, sweet Mina, not only my heart rejoices —

MINA.   *(Laughing.)* Lucy, you're mad —

LUCY.   Oh, but oh so much more of me! You fill me up with solicitous longings!

MINA.   *(Playing along.)* Not till we're married, I've told you! *(Mina pushes Lucy from the bed. Lucy rushes to the window and playfully "clothes" herself in the long black drapes.)*

LUCY.   Married in the eyes of whom?

MINA.   In the eyes of the moon —!

LUCY.   — Which is rich and full of permission, now what do you say?

MINA.   *(A quick pause, a naughty look.)* Come and let me have the all of you!

LUCY.   Mina! *(Lucy rushes to her. They throw the sheet over them and wrestle on the bed, as — a Maid enters.)*

MAID.   Miss Lucy.

LUCY.   *(Still under the sheet.)* Go away, I'm dead!

MAID.   Miss Lucy, that gentleman is here again. *(All motion under the sheet stops. Lucy pokes her head up. Then Mina does the*

same, turns to Lucy.)
MINA. What gentleman?
MAID. Mister Seward, the doctor.
MINA. A doctor! Lucy...!
MAID. What should I tell him?
LUCY. Tell him to come back tomorrow. I am indisposed.
MAID. Very well.
MINA. *(To Lucy.)* Why didn't you tell me?!
LUCY. And do open the window on your way out. How many times must I ask you? *(The Maid nods, apologetically, then opens the window — faint sound of crashing waves, as the Maid leaves. Mina looks at Lucy, who gazes out the window.)*
MINA. No secrets, Lucy. That's what we've always said to one another, since we were children. There must be a bond of trust between us. *(Lucy turns to her.)* Tell me.
LUCY. Oh, Mina, can't you guess? I am in love! (I needn't tell you this secret must not leave this room.) I am in love, Mina! Oh, how bountiful is the world and how true are the proverbs.
MINA. The proverbs?
LUCY. It never rains but it pours. Mina, I am not indisposed ... I am undecided.
MINA. Whether to marry him or not?
LUCY. No. Which one of them to marry.
MINA. There is more than one?
LUCY. Three! Three suitors. Me, who all these years never had even *one!* Two of them have already proposed —
MINA. Who? *(Lucy shows Mina small, framed photos of each of the men.)*
LUCY. Mr. Holmwood, the judge; and Mr. Morris, the Texan.
MINA. Does he have horses?
LUCY. Horses are the least of what he has.
MINA. Lucy —!
LUCY. And now, Dr. Seward — only twenty-nine and already in control of an immense lunatic asylum. He is versed in the arts of dream interpretation and *hypnosis!* Oh, I can fancy what a wonderful power he must have over his patients.
MINA. Lucy, what will you do?

LUCY.   Why can't they let a girl marry three men and save all this trouble? Yes, I know, that is heresy and I must not say it — but, dear Mina, all this happiness has made me so utterly miserable ... *(She breaks down and cries, as Mina holds and comforts her.)*

MINA.   Oh, sweet Lucy. Hold tight and have hope. My love is away, your loves are too near. We shall mingle our tears together. *(A shaft of light on Harker. His coat is off, his sleeves are rolled up. He holds some papers. He sips from a silver goblet. Faint sound of wolves howling, trees rustling.)*

HARKER.   My dear Mina, what a place I am in! Mr. Dawkins never let on what a grand job he had assigned to me. I must thank him on my return. The carriage came as scheduled, the coachman loaded my things in silence and took off into the night. The cold air was pierced by the thrilling call of wolves — seemingly *hundreds* of them. And, in fact, when I lit a match to look at my watch, the reflection on the carriage window gave the illusion of hundreds of pairs of red eyes, staring from the hillsides around me. It gave me a wonderful fright! When we reached the castle, I tried but failed to see the coachman's face. He lifted all my belongings with a single hand and when I mentioned the swiftness of his horses, his only reply was: "The dead travel fast." For his part, the Count was ever so cordial, and, seeing my fatigue, led me directly to this room. It is well-appointed, and not unlike a home in England except for the complete absence of mirrors. We could learn, I'm sure, from this noble absence of vanity. *(Lucy's Sitting Room. Noon. Lucy is checking her face in a small hand mirror, as — Seward enters and appears behind him. Lucy sees him first in the mirror.)*

LUCY.   Hello, Dr. Seward.

SEWARD.   Do call me John, won't you? *(Lucy nods, and turns to him, setting the mirror down. Seward approaches her.)* I'm sorry I disturbed you yesterday. It was impulsive of me.

LUCY.   Not at all. I was —

SEWARD.   Indisposed. The maid told me.

LUCY.   Sickly, actually.

SEWARD.   In what way? A fever?

LUCY.   Yes, a fever.

SEWARD.   And now? Are you feeling better now?

LUCY.   I don't know. Am I? *(She stands. He stares at her, then steps in. He gently feels her forehead. She closes her eyes at his touch. His hands gracefully and gently move to her neck, continuing to check her. Then, he steps back. Her eyes remain closed.)* Well?

SEWARD.   There is but one thing out of the ordinary.

LUCY.   And what is that?

SEWARD.   Your incomparable beauty. *(She opens her eyes. She stares at him, speechless.)* You are not ill, Lucy. It is I who carry an illness. It eats away at me day and night, and its only remedy resides in the very heart which afflicts me. Your heart. *(Pause.)* May I speak? *(Thrilled, stunned, she nods ... then sits.)* My dear Lucy, let me say it out loud: I work with lunatics. An amusing statement, yes, a cavalier admission in the eyes of the world — but the world does not see what I see. Each day, in ways too intricate to mention, I glimpse the mad souls of men. And from this I have learned the following: we have, all of us, a secret life. And though we are loathe to *divulge* it, we do, on occasion, grant *access.* We do, in rare and remarkable ways, allow one person proximity to our hidden self. What I know of you, Lucy, is terribly dear to me. What I will never know of you, is dearer still. *(He kneels.)* So, please. Accept me, and be cherished above all women. Bid me stay, and be, to your final days, adored. *(She begins to cry, softly. He watches for a moment, then leaps to his feet.)* Oh, that I be struck dumb! That I be swept away to sea and pummeled into driftwood! My sweet, kind-hearted Lucy: I am a brute! I am carrion for vultures and worms! I have wrought tears in the very eyes where I least intended them. *(She looks up at him.)* You cannot love me at present. That is the clear and stinging prognosis and I must accept it. But, tell me: dare I hope? Could you *learn* to love me, in time? *(She cries again, very softly.)* There is someone already. Your heart, making way for your hand, is previously betrothed. Am I right, dear Lucy? *(She looks up at him. She is, perhaps, about to answer, as — Seward nods.)* I feared that. Two forever gain at the loss of a third. *(He goes to her, offers his hand, lifts her to her feet. Looks in her eyes. Speaks with resolute clarity.)* Hear me now: from this moment on, your happiness is my fondest wish. If your heart was free, a man might have hope. But, in place of hope, I give you something far stronger and eminently wiser: I give you my friendship. And, whatever you need of it shall be yours for the asking. *(Pause.)* And from you, if I might have a remembrance. Something like your mirror, which has held your image as vividly as I. *(She lifts the small mirror and hands it to him. She looks in his eyes. She leans forward and* <u>*kisses him*</u>*, very gently, on the lips. He closes his eyes. She looks at him. He opens his eyes, speaks softly.)* That kiss, sweet Lucy, that will be something to keep off the darkness. *(He steps back, looks at her ... then leaves, taking the mirror with him. Lucy cries and rushes to the window, looking out, as — Lights isolate Seward, alone, opposite. He takes off his jacket and rolls up his sleeves, speaking with precision and calm.)* That is done, then. We have been rebuffed. The world is empty. There is nothing worth doing. Fortunately, there is one way in which a lost love can be revenged: at the hand of one's work. *(He screams with a manic intensity.)* RENFIELD! *(He rushes across the stage and arrives at — Renfield's cell. The asylum. Renfield is busily making notations in a crude notebook, as he quickly counts the numerous tiny [unseen] life forms in his cell. He is always* <u>*chained at the ankle*</u> *unless otherwise noted. A sparrow flies around inside a crude birdcage. Two Attendants are nearby. One reads a newspaper. One is asleep.)*

RENFIELD.   *(To himself.)* Yes good yes yes good yes very good yes good good yes very good yes yes ... *(As Renfield continues, Seward rushes up to the Attendants, who straighten up, immediately.)*

SEWARD.   How is he?

ATTENDANT ONE.   Quite well, sir.

ATTENDANT TWO.   On his best behavior.

ATTENDANT ONE.   Not a thing out of the ordinary. *(Incensed, Seward throws them out of his way.)*

SEWARD.   I told you to keep him to his madness! How can I study him if you allow him to revert to his sanity?! *(Before they can answer —)* GET OUT OF MY SIGHT. *(The Attendants leave, as — Seward approaches Renfield, who does not look up.)*

RENFIELD.   You've been crying.

SEWARD.   What?

RENFIELD.   Mind your step. There is life there.

SEWARD. The spiders have nearly doubled.

RENFIELD. I lure them, I house them, the world feeds on the carcass of itself, may I smell you? Please please. *(Seward steps back.)* Salt, I think. Salt and perfume. You, too, have been in the presence of life. *(Renfield instantly smashes his open palm against Seward's chest.)*

SEWARD. For god's sake — *(Renfield pulls his palm away and peels a large, dead fly from Seward's shirt. Holds it up.)*

RENFIELD. And life tastes good, doesn't it Johnny? *(Renfield eats the fly. Seward watches, though it disgusts him.)*

SEWARD. You've trained the sparrow, I see.

RENFIELD. Yes, a good bird, that. Why won't she marry you?

SEWARD. What are you talking about?

RENFIELD. I should brood if I were you. I should brood and think of sporadic killings. *(Quickly back to his notebook.)* Yes yes good yes good yes very good yes yes yes ... *(Seward watches him for a moment, then steps toward him.)*

SEWARD. But, why, Renfield? Why the eating of flies and spiders?

RENFIELD. I have a great love for animals.

SEWARD. No evasions today, I'm not of a mood. Now, again —

RENFIELD. They are life. And they give life to me. I absorb it through them, blood running into blood.

SEWARD. *(Reaching out his hand.)* And the notebook?

RENFIELD. *(Holding the notebook tightly to his chest.)* NO.

SEWARD. You must have a plan of some kind.

RENFIELD. NO.

SEWARD. First the flies, then the spiders, then the sparrow, you have a PLAN —

RENFIELD. NO.

SEWARD. I shall solve you, Renfield. You are a life-eating maniac and I shall solve the secret of your mind! I am not afraid of the world's rampant complacency. To question is to discover. Men sneered at vivisection, and yet look at its results today! Why not, therefore, advance science in its most difficult and vital aspect — the BRAIN? For if I held the key to JUST ONE LUNATIC, I might advance my own branch of science to such lofty esteem that Burdon-Sanderson's physiology would be as NOTHING —

RENFIELD. And Miss Lucy would give her hand.

SEWARD. SHUT UP!

RENFIELD. *(Sweetly.)* May I have a kitten?

SEWARD. What?!

RENFIELD. A kitten, please please. A nice little playful kitten, that I can ... play with, and ... teach, and ... feed and feed and feed. No one would refuse me a kitten, would they?

SEWARD. How is it you know her name? *(Renfield quickly turns away, grabs the bird cage and begins singing a tiny little song to the sparrow.)*

RENFIELD.
Bird-blood feather-blood spider-blood fly-blood,
Bird-blood feather-blood spider-blood fly-blood ...

SEWARD. Tell me! *(Seward grabs Renfield by the shoulder and turns him. This is the first time we have seen him touch Renfield. Renfield wheels around, viciously, fire in his eyes, his jaw clenched, ready to fight, as — Seward takes a step back.)* Miss Lucy. How do you know her name?

RENFIELD. My Master.

SEWARD. What?

RENFIELD. My Master told me. *(Crash of thunder and rush of music as lights shift to — A silhouette of Dracula, far U., his arms extended, his cape opened, bat. . rom the silhouette, a pair of red eyes [perhaps] glowing in the darkness. We do not see his face. A great burst of smoke — another crash of th der/music, and — in an instant, the silhouette is gone. In its place is — Harker, in a shaft of light, looking terrified and haggard, h   ' s rumpled. He wears the rosary around his neck. He speaks with urgency from the billowing smoke and forbidding darkness. Sound of bats shrieking, doors slamming shut.)*

HARKER. Sweet Mina! I am all in a sea of wonders. I think strange things which I dare not confess to mine own soul! There is something of a nightmare about this place and I fear my superstitions may run riot within me. And the Count, my host: what manner of man is this?! I feel the dread of his presence overwhelming me. I am encompassed about with terrors

18

that I dare not think of ... *(The storm breaks wide open, filling the theatre with sound and fury, as lights shift to — Lucy's bedroom. Night. A full moon out the window. Lightning illuminating the dark room at random intervals. Lucy and Mina asleep in the bed, as the storm rages. A wolf howls, in the distance. Suddenly, Lucy stirs. She sits up. She rises from the bed, sleepwalking, and moves toward the window. She throws wide the drapes. She touches the window very lightly with her fingers, as though caressing it. Then ... she <u>presses her entire body flush against the window</u>. She writhes with pleasure, as though in the grasp of the window itself. A wicked crack of thunder — Mina wakes. Sees the empty bed. Sees Lucy by the window.)*

MINA.   Lucy, come to bed. *(No reaction.)* Lucy, it's just a dream. You're sleepwalking again. Come back to bed. *(Still no reaction. Mina, stands, putting on a robe. She lifts Lucy's robe from the bed and carries it toward Lucy.)* The storm has frightened you. You're having another dream. Come morning, it will all be gone. *(Mina walks to Lucy and gently pulls her a few steps away from the window. Lucy continues to look out. Mina places the robe around her shoulders, as — the howl of a wolf joins the sound of the storm. Lucy suddenly throws off the robe and rushes back to the window again.)* Lucy, what is it? What's there? *(Lucy jumps onto the window sill, as Mina tries to pull her back to bed.)*

LUCY.   The waves are wild! The ship is tossed about!

MINA.   Lucy, you're scaring me. Come down from there —

LUCY.   But fear not, the ship will find its port. The ship will best the storm!

MINA.   There are no ships, Lucy. None would be out on a night like this —

LUCY.   There it is! Riding the waves! Pounding about on the blood of the earth! *(Lights shift quickly to — Renfield's cell. Renfield, shirtless, is alternately leaping about in a fervor — and quickly cleaning himself in the exact manner of a <u>cat</u>. Seward rushes on, furious, and encounters a frantic Attendant. The Attendant holds a straitjacket. The storm continues. Mina and Lucy remain lit, in tableau.)*

RENFIELD.   IT IS HE! HE HAS COME FOR ME! THE MASTER HAS COME!

SEWARD.   What on earth is he —

19

ATTENDANT. The storm, I think, it set him off somehow —
SEWARD. Renfield! What is it?
RENFIELD. MY MASTER GROWS NEAR!
SEWARD. Who are you talking about?
RENFIELD. *(With an odd, lucid calm.)* The bride-maidens re-
joice the coming of the bride; but when the bride draweth
nigh, the maidens shine not.
ATTENDANT. I think he's had a reckoning. I think he's
found God!
SEWARD. I pray not. Homicidal mania and religious fervor
would be a dangerous combination. *(Moving in closer, seeing
Renfield cleaning himself.)* Renfield, what are you doing?
RENFIELD. I must be clean for my Master.
SEWARD. Your flies are gone. And the spiders are gone,
also. *(No reaction.)* Look at me. Where have they gone? And
what of your sparrow? Where is it? *(Renfield reaches into his
mouth and coughs, producing — A sparrow feather, which flutters
to the ground.)* My god. *(He turns to the Attendant.)* BIND HIM!
NOW! *(Flash of lightning/huge thunder crack, as a shaft of light
reveals — Harker. His clothes look like rags — torn and filthy. He
speaks wildly, sodden with dementia and fear. Sound of a high-pitched
ringing joins the sound of the storm.)*
HARKER. The digging! All day and night the digging, the
constant digging! Oh, my far-away, Mina — if only I knew what
it all meant! Great wooden boxes have been hauled away —
and for what reason? I fear I am the only living soul within
this place, and everywhere I turn: doors, doors, doors everywhere — all locked and bolted! I am a prisoner! *(A blinding
flash of lightning/severe crack of thunder which suddenly reveals all
three areas at once: Harker — still struggling to speak, as we see
something slithering around near his legs. It is, in fact, the Two Vixens — two women with deathly pale skin, wild hair, clad in white,
flowing, diaphanous rags. We do not, however, see their faces. During the following, they climb, vine-like, up Harker's legs — wrapping
their limbs about him. Lucy and Mina — Lucy throws the window
open and leans out into the storm, as Mina tries to hold onto her,
to save her. Seward and Renfield — as the Attendant tries to bind
Renfield, Renfield uses the straitjacket to snap the man's neck, kill-*

ing him instantly. Seward looks on, helpless, horrified — Through-
out, a manic cacophony of sound: the storm, the wolves, the bats,
the high-pitched screeching.)

HARKER.
And now I know,
Mina! Now I
know what the
digging was for!
And now I know
what I must do: I
must rid the
world of such
monsters! They
are the devils of
the Pit! I shall es-
cape, Mina —
away from this
cursed land! And
if I fail, goodbye,
sweet Mina!
Goodbye my one
true love! Re-
member me and
keep me in your
prayers!

GOODBYE!

MINA.
Lucy, no!

LUCY.
I want to see the
ship!

MINA.
No — take my
hand — it's not
safe!

LUCY.
Look, he's come
for me!

MINA.
Lucy, stop it —
you're dream-
ing!

LUCY.
I'M HERE! I'M
HERE!

SEWARD.
Renfield, let him
go!

RENFIELD.
He should have
been nice to me!
Now, he's my
pet. I'll call him
Tabby.

SEWARD.
You'll be punished,
I promise you!

RENFIELD.
My Master will pro-
tect me! Listen to
the wind — listen
to it howl! HE IS
NEAR, say the
waves! THE MAS-
TER! THE MAS-
TER IS AT HAND!

(As the music and storm crescendo — Harker has been overcome by
the slithering Vixens. Lucy has hurled Mina back onto the bed. Lucy
leans out the window, silhouetted against the enormous full moon.
Seward rushes away from Renfield, who pets the dead Attendant.
Then, suddenly, all light vanishes but a small shaft, D. Music and
storm snap out. All is silent. There, in the dim light is … a large
wooden box, coffin-sized. We stare at the box in silence for a long
while. Then … it shakes a bit, just the tiniest bit. Just a hint of
something within. A pause. A bit more shaking. Then, the shaking

stops. Another silence. Then ... slowly ... creakily ... the <u>lid to the</u> <u>box begins to open</u>. As it does, lights snap out. Music from the dark-ness, then lights up, revealing — a ship's wheel, weathered, stand-ing alone, attached only to a few battered planks of the ship. And, tied by its hands to the wheel with a string of rosary beads ... a full human skeleton. Hideous, and still wet; mud and seaweed amid the bones. A man, his back to us, stands looking at the skeleton, shak-ing his head with sadness. [This is Dracula — dressed <u>exactly</u> as Harker.] <u>We do not clearly see Dracula's face.</u> Seward, wearing a warm coat, enters. It is nearly dawn.)

SEWARD.   It's just as they said.

DRACULA.   Yes.

SEWARD.   What could have — *(Stops.)* No. It's too horrible to think of. Did any of the crew survive?

DRACULA.   Only a dog, they say.

SEWARD.   A dog?

DRACULA.   A large grey dog which leapt from the ship. Or, so they say.

SEWARD.   A wonder it even made it to port in a storm like that.

DRACULA.   A miracle.

SEWARD.   Pardon my manners, I don't believe I know you. I'm John Seward.

DRACULA.   *(Pause, he turns to Seward.)* You head the asylum, do you not?

SEWARD.   Yes, I do. And you are?

DRACULA.   Harker. Jonathan Harker. *(They shake hands. Seward takes note of the coldness of Dracula's hand.)*

SEWARD.   Well, Mr. Harker. A true pleasure. I've heard of you from Miss Lucy Westenra. You're engaged, I believe, to her friend Mina.

DRACULA.   Yes. And you to Miss Lucy? *(Pause, Seward stares at him.)* I'm told she's very beautiful. *(Silence.)*

SEWARD.   How odd to meet you here.

DRACULA.   *(With an odd chill.)* Where would you have us meet?

SEWARD.   *(A pause.)* Well. Yes. You're right. Good to, though, finally. *(Dracula gently touches the cheek of the skeleton.)*

DRACULA. He was a righteous man. Is this, you suppose, what happens to righteous men?

SEWARD. And this fact the strangest: he lashed himself to the wheel with his own rosary.

DRACULA. *(As he takes a small step backward.)* Yes.

SEWARD. We'll never know, will we?

DRACULA. That depends, I suppose.

SEWARD. How do you mean?

DRACULA. On what you're hoping to know. *(Tips his hat.)* Good day. *(Dracula goes, as, behind him, the sun begins to rise. Seward watches him leave, as lights shift to — Lucy's bedroom. Morning. Lucy lies in the bed, a cloth across her forehead, her face very pale. Mina sits on the bed next to her, holding her hand.)*

LUCY. And then?

MINA. I've told you enough.

LUCY. No, Mina. I must know.

MINA. Then ... I found you on the cliff, lying amid the rocks. It's a wonder you didn't fall. I wrapped you in a blanket and brought you home.

LUCY. Mina —

MINA. You're fine, now. And safe. I've sent for Dr. Seward.

LUCY. Mina, listen to me. You must, as my dearest friend, promise me this: that you'll tell no one of these odd events. Even my family. Promise me.

MINA. *(After a pause, touching Lucy's face.)* I promise. *(Lucy smiles a bit, holds Mina's hand.)*

LUCY. And what of you? What is the news from Jonathan?

MINA. There is no news. A fortnight and still no word from him. *(The Maid escorts Seward into the room. He carries a leather doctor's bag.)*

MAID. Dr. Seward, ma'am.

SEWARD. Good morning, ladies. You must be Mina. *(Mina rises and moves to him, away from Lucy.)*

MINA. Thank you for coming. Lucy commends your skill as a doctor.

SEWARD. More minds have I treated than bodies, but I'll do what I can. How is she?

MINA. Weak. And very pale. Please — *(Mina gestures to the*

bed. Seward moves close to Lucy.)

SEWARD.   Hello, Lucy.

LUCY.   Hello, again. *(He checks her pulse, eyes, heart, etc. during the following.)*

SEWARD.   When did this begin?

LUCY.   The storm last night. I slept poorly.

SEWARD.   Bad dreams?

LUCY.   *(The truth.)* Yes.

SEWARD.   Can you tell me?

LUCY.   It's very vague.

MINA.   Try, Lucy.

LUCY.   There was a ... howling. A dog howling —

SEWARD.   *(Simply.)* A dog —

LUCY.   Or many of them, hundreds or more, as though the whole town were full of them. And I seemed to be sinking into deep water, green water, and there was a singing in my ears. And then — *(She stops.)*

SEWARD.   Go on.

LUCY.   And then ... something very sweet and very bitter all around me at once ... and I felt everything passing away from me ... my soul seemed to go out of my body and float about in the air. And then — *(At this moment, Seward has turned her head and is looking at something on her <u>neck</u> — which we cannot see. A brief, still moment, as — a church bell tolls, beautifully, in the distance. Lucy turns her head and looks up at Seward. Seward removes his hand from her neck. Then, Lucy looks to Mina.)* And then Mina woke me. And told me I'd been dreaming. *(Seward looks at Lucy for a long time.)*

MINA.   Dr. Seward, what is it?

SEWARD.   *(To Lucy.)* There is a mark on your neck.

LUCY.   A mark?

SEWARD.   A red mark. As though you'd been kissed there. *(Pause, now the hint of jealousy.)* Have you been?

LUCY.   *(Touching his face, tenderly.)* No, John.

SEWARD.   *(Pause, then standing.)* I'll begin with your blood.

LUCY.   My blood?

SEWARD.   I'll assess its qualities. To discover any malady that may reside within. *(Seward takes a small, pointed tool, and a small glass container from his bag. A small jar of ointment, as well. Lucy looks to Mina, who sits on the bed to comfort her.)*

MINA.   Do as he says, now. Don't be frightened.

SEWARD.   Miss Lucy ...

LUCY.   Yes?

SEWARD.   May I have your hand? *(Silence. Lucy smiles a bit, then offers her hand to him. He takes her hand. He rubs a small bit of ointment on her finger. He pricks her finger, quickly, with the tool. Lucy looks down at the blood. He squeezes her finger, gently, until a few drops of blood fall into the glass container.)* There we are. If you'll wrap that, Mina. *(Mina wraps a small white cloth around Lucy's finger, as Seward seals up the dish.)*

LUCY.   John.

SEWARD.   Yes?

LUCY.   You are my true friend. *(Seward nods, saying nothing, as — the Maid enters.)*

MAID.   Miss Mina, a letter has arrived for you. Shall I bring it in?

MINA.   From where is it posted?

MAID.   From a hospital, ma'am. In Budapest. *(Mina stands, urgently.)*

MINA.   I'll be right there.

LUCY.   Mina, I pray the news is —

MINA.   Ssshh. Save your strength. I'll see you when you wake. *(Seward and Mina walk away from the bed.)* I thank you, Dr. Seward.

SEWARD.   Keep a watchful eye. And don't let her leave this room.

MINA.   I won't.

SEWARD.   Miss Mina, if I may — *(Mina stops, looks at him.)* — you are as remarkable as Lucy described.

MINA.   As are you, Dr. Seward.

SEWARD.   Early today, I had the pleasure of meeting Mr. Harker, your fiancé. He seems a fine man. *(She stares at him.)* What is it?

MINA.   That's impossible. He's out of the country.

SEWARD.   Well, perhaps I —

MINA.   *(Sharply.)* Till just now, I've had no word in weeks.

25

Why would you say such a thing?

SEWARD. Miss Mina — *(She is gone. He looks off after her, then looks back at Lucy.)*

LUCY. I'm so warm, John. Won't you open the window? *(Seward moves to the window, as lights shift to — an entryway. Evening. A Maid turns in her work, and is startled to see the man [Dracula, as Harker] we saw earlier. He wears a cape now. His back is to her, and to us. An odd, distant sound — something like the high-pitched ringing of glassware.)*

MAID. Oh! *(A good laugh now.)* I'm sorry, sir. May I help you?

DRACULA. Say it.

MAID. I beg your —

DRACULA. *(Not turning around.)* This is the home of Miss Lucy, is it not?

MAID. Aye, it is, but —

DRACULA. *(Quietly.)* Say it. *(Silence. The Maid stares at him, curious.)* You're very beautiful. *(Silence. The Maid stares at him, more serious now ...)* You know that. Don't you? *(The Maid stares at him, flattered, growing shy ...)* Please. Do what I'm thinking. *(The Maid stares at him, becoming frightened now ...)* Say it. *(She takes a deep breath, unable to take her eyes off Dracula. He nods, prompting her.)*

MAID. You. May. Enter. *(The man turns, with a flourish — and we see Dracula for the first time. Youthful and vibrant, sensual and charismatic. He smiles a beautiful smile.)*

DRACULA. Remember me, won't you?

MAID. *(Breathlessly.)* Oh, yes.

DRACULA. Good. *(She gestures "come in" .... He smiles. He does not enter. Instead, he turns, flashing his cape, and leaves the way he came in. Lights shift to — a sanitarium. A simple white chair will suffice. Harker sits, wearing a white robe, his head bandaged. He does nothing but stare forward in a horrific daze. Mina rushes in. She carries a small bag. She begins to hug him, but stops, shocked by the sight of him.)*

MINA. Jonathan? *(No response, silence.)* I took a boat to Hamburg as soon as I heard. And then the train here. *(Still no response, still more silence.)* They say you've had a terrible shock, that you're suffering from a violent brain fever. *(Still nothing. Mina kneels, takes his hand, begins to cry softly.)* Oh, Jonathan, your eyes. All resolution, all light has gone from them. Please tell me. What has happened? *(Her head is in his lap as she cries. He slowly lifts his hand and places it gently on her head. Feeling this, she looks up, taking his hand, kissing it.)* They say in a few days you'll be well enough to travel. They've given me your things, but I couldn't find your briefcase among them. Only this — *(She removes a leather-bound journal from her bag. He turns and looks at the journal. She begins to open the journal.)* — And I'm not sure whether this is — *(He puts his hand down on top of hers with force, shutting the journal. She looks up at him, confused, frightened.)* — Jonathan?

HARKER.   *(An urgent, somber voice.)* Mina. We have spoken of trust between a husband and a wife. That there should be no secrets, no concealment between us. I have been driven mad. But amid this tortu̅ ̅, one gift: the loss of memory. I've no idea what happened to bring me here. I've no idea which things were real and which were the insidious dreams of a madman. The secret is here, in my journal. Take it. Keep it. Read it, if you must — but *never let me know.* I do not want to return to those bitter hours, those ghastly days. So, unless solemn duty bids you do otherwise, keep this to your heart only. And may this secret prove the final one between us, so long as we two shall be as one. *(She stares at him. She removes a <u>blue ribbon</u> from around her neck. She ties the ribbon around the journal, binding it <u>closed</u>.)*

MINA.   *(Very softly.)* It's done. Let's go home. *(He takes the rosary from around his neck and holds it out to her. She stares at it, curious, as it dangles from his fingers. Music, as lights shift to — Lucy's bedroom. Night. The moon, of course, is full and high, flooding the room with light. The drapes are parted. The window is partly open. Lucy is asleep. A clock is chiming midnight. And now ... the piercing howl of a wolf, nearby. Lucy stirs. Another howl. Lucy sits up. She puts a robe on over her nightgown. She is sleepwalking again. She leaves the bed and walks — with her arms at her sides — to the window. As she approaches the window, the huge head of a grey wolf rises up into sight, outside the window [or: a silhouette* *or projection of a wolf is seen, upstage.] It howls again. Lucy, head still down, does not seem to see the wolf. She throws the window wide open. The sound of waves crashing is heard. Lucy takes off her robe and casts it out the window, into the sea. As she does this, the wolf's eyes [perhaps] begin to <u>glow red</u>. Then, still casually, still sleepwalking ... Lucy <u>closes</u> the window. As she does this, the wolf's head slowly <u>disappears</u>. The <u>red eyes vanish</u>. Lucy takes hold of one side of the black drapes — and pulls it <u>closed</u>. She then takes hold of the <u>other side</u> of the black drapes and pulls it — but it is, in fact — <u>Dracula's cape</u>. She is now engulfed in his arms.)*

DRACULA.   Good evening. *(Lucy screams, coming instantly awake.)* Don't be frightened.

LUCY.   MOTHER!

DRACULA.   Your mother is indisposed. As are the servants.

LUCY.   Mina, HELP ME!

DRACULA.   And Miss Mina, too, is gone. We're alone, sweet Lucy. *(He releases her. She backs away from him, slowly, covering a spot on her neck with her hands.)* Your friend, Dr. Seward, has examined your blood and found it to be rich and healthy. *(He licks his lips.)* I share his diagnosis. *(Music, as — Lucy rushes to the window and throws it open. Instantly, Dracula <u>points</u> to the window — and it <u>slams shut</u>, of its own accord. Lucy pounds against the window, crying. Then, exhausted, she turns back to him, terrified.)*

LUCY.   What are you? What do you want of me? *(He approaches her slowly, calmly.)*

DRACULA.   I want your fear. For your fear, like a current, rushes through your body. Your fear makes your heart pound, it renders your veins rich and full. Your fear hemorrhages deliciously within you. *(He is leaning over her. He speaks softly, and very kindly.)* Do what I'm thinking. *(Her eyes transfixed on his, she slowly pulls back her long red hair ... exposing her neck. Offering it to him. He lowers his mouth to her neck very slowly, like a quiet kiss. <u>He bites her, very gently</u>, once ... making her body tense and shiver. He lifts his head and looks in her eyes. She looks up at him. In the distance, we begin to see hundreds of pairs of red eyes, glowing in the darkness.)* It's only a dream, Lucy. You've been sleepwalking again. And dear Mina shall keep your secret.

When you wake, you shall remember only the cry of a wolf, and the crash of the sea. *(He looks down at her neck, achingly. Then ... in one ravenous motion ... he hurls his head down onto her neck — lights instantly snap out, as — Lucy screams, and, simultaneously, we hear Renfield scream from the darkness — as lights rise on — Renfield's cell. He is now chained at the wrist [as well as the ankle] to the walls/bars of his cell. He screams, wildly, struggling to get free.)*

RENFIELD. I AM HERE, MASTER! I AM HERE TO DO YOUR BIDDING! NOW THAT YOU ARE NEAR, I AWAIT YOUR COMMANDS! *(Seward rushes in.)*

SEWARD. Renfield, what is it?!

RENFIELD. *(Paying Seward no mind.)* AND I PRAY YOU: DO NOT PASS ME BY, DEAR MASTER —

SEWARD. *(Overlapping slightly.)* Who are you talking to —?!

RENFIELD. WHEN YOU DISTRIBUTE YOUR GLORIOUS TIDINGS, PLEASE, DO NOT PASS ME BY! *(In an instant, Renfield turns to Seward, cheerfully, as though nothing whatsoever had happened.)* You're out late.

SEWARD. What, yes, listen to me now —

RENFIELD. And though she's promised to another, you keep watch. You maintain an avid readiness.

SEWARD. I am not —

RENFIELD. But, we can wait, can't we Johnny? Clever men that we are. We can wait for the riches to fill our cup. *(An instant rage, looking up.)* DO NOT FORGET ME! *(An instant, lucid calm, back to Seward.)* We are one man, Johnny. We host a common longing. You await her deep mysteries, as I await my Master's gifts.

SEWARD. *(Going into the cell.)* I will SOLVE YOU, Renfield. I shall unearth the mad logic of your mind. Now, I demand to know: WHO IS YOUR MASTER?

RENFIELD. We are men at the mercy of angels. *(An Attendant rushes in.)*

ATTENDANT. Dr. Seward —

SEWARD. Not now —

ATTENDANT. It's Miss Lucy, sir. She's — *(And before the Attendant can finish, Seward is out of the room. The Attendant turns and looks at Renfield, who smiles and says [or: he mouths the words as we hear Dracula's amplified voice say].)*

RENFIELD.   The unexpected always happens. *(Lights shift instantly to a small area D., where — Van Helsing stands, his back to us, reading from a letter. Next to him is a small valise. He turns to the audience as he reads aloud.)*

VAN HELSING.   "You are my friend and master, and you know more about obscure diseases than anyone in the world. You are a philosopher and metaphysician and the most advanced scientist of your day. You have an absolutely open mind, an iron nerve, a temper of ice, an indomitable resolution, and the kindliest and truest heart that beats. These things provide the equipment for the noble work which you are doing for the good of mankind. I entreat you now, with an all-embracing humility, to come to the aid of my dear, sweet Lucy." *(Stops reading, looks up at the audience.)* To be clear: I am not a slave to flattery. A man's reputation is the most imperfect science of all. *(Smiles a bit.)* I, for one, would love to meet the man whom young Dr. Seward describes. *(Looks at the letter.)* No, what swayed me was the blunt accuracy of his postscript. *(Reads.)* "P.S. Do remember that I once saved your life." *(Lights expand, revealing — Lucy's bedroom. Day. Lucy lies in bed, extremely pale, very weak. She is half-awake, her breathing is labored. Around her neck is a scarf. Seward sits by her side, holding her limp hand. Van Helsing walks into the room, heading directly for Lucy.)*

SEWARD.   It's as though she is fading away. Every day more pale, gasping for air.

VAN HELSING.   Miss Lucy, can you hear me? *(Lucy opens her eyes.)* I am Abraham Van Helsing. I have come from Amsterdam at Dr. Seward's request. I must ask you a question or two. Would that be all right? *(Lucy nods.)* Good. Now, have you had a fall, lately? Or a fright of some kind, anything out of the ordinary?

LUCY.   Only the dreams.

VAN HELSING.   Tell me.

LUCY.   Oh, I tried not to sleep. I tried so hard not to fall asleep —

SEWARD.   Why, Lucy?

LUCY. *(Sitting up in the bed.)* And, yet, I *must* have slept — because the clock struck twelve and woke me. There was a scratching, a flapping of something at the window. What could that have been?

SEWARD. The wind, I suspect. A rustle of trees —

VAN HELSING. And the dreams? What do you remember of them?

LUCY. A wolf. The cry of a wolf. And the sound of the sea.

VAN HELSING. Anything else?

LUCY. *(The truth.)* Only that. *(Silence.)*

VAN HELSING. Here. Lie back. Rest now. *(As Van Helsing helps her lie back into bed, her scarf comes loosely away from her neck, and — Van Helsing notices something on her neck. He turns to Seward.)* Who has access to this room?

SEWARD. *(Thinking the question odd.)* Only myself, her mother, and the maid.

VAN HELSING. I'll want to speak to them. Don't ask, just yet — but trust me, there may be cause. There is always cause for everything. *(He takes a small bottle of liquid from his valise, pours a bit of it into a glass, then stirs a small amount of powder into it. He turns to Lucy.)* Miss Lucy, I'd like you to drink this. It's a bit of brandy and a sleeping aid — it will help you rest.

LUCY. I don't want to sleep. I'd rather *die* than ever sleep again. This weakness comes to me in my dreams, and I am unclean, I feel as if there is no air, no air at all, as if there was —

VAN HELSING. Ssshh. Quiet.

LUCY. You must wake me from my dreams!

VAN HELSING. Quiet, now. We shall keep you safe. Now, drink this and rest. *(Lucy looks at him, then drinks from the glass and lies back in the bed.)*

SEWARD. I'll be here, Lucy. I shan't leave you. *(She closes her eyes, as — Van Helsing ushers Seward away from the bed, urgently.)* What is it?

VAN HELSING. She wants blood, my friend. And blood she must have or she will die. Roll up your sleeve. There is no time to waste. *(Van Helsing begins taking the necessary equipment out of his valise.)*

31

SEWARD. *(Looking at the equipment.)* I've never seen such instruments.

VAN HELSING. The ghastly paraphernalia of our beneficial trade. *(Giving him a cloth doused in alcohol.)* Swab your arm with this. *(Seward does as told, as Van Helsing does the same to Lucy's arm. During the following, Van Helsing inserts the transfusion device into their arms, connecting them via a <u>long, thin tube</u> — then turns a lever on a small pump which begins the transfer of blood. [If possible, we see the tube go from clear to <u>blood-red</u>.])*

SEWARD. She fears her dreams, but dreaming alone cannot render such havoc. I remember nothing from my studies that ever spoke of such a —

VAN HELSING. Remember, friend, that knowledge is stronger than memory, and we should not trust the weaker. (Lift your arm a degree. Good.) The case of our dear miss is one that may be — mind, I say *may be* — of such interest that we may generate new and vital knowledge regarding the canon of catastrophe. Take then good note of it. Nothing is too small. I counsel you, put down in record even your doubts and surmises.

SEWARD. You speak as if formulating a theory —

VAN HELSING. (Ah, be this not love in its purest sense? To transfer from full veins of one to empty veins of another.) — Now, my good friend John, this word of caution: You deal with madmen. All men are mad in some way or the other, and inasmuch as you deal *discreetly* with *your* madmen, so, too, you must deal with *God's* madmen.

SEWARD. Who might they be?

VAN HELSING. The rest of the world. You and I must *keep knowledge in its place.* We must keep what we learn here — *(Touches Seward on the heart.)* and here — *(Touches him on the forehead.)* — and trust only one another with these secrets.

SEWARD. You speak as though playing a game.

VAN HELSING. I assure you, John, there is no jest here. Only life and death ... and perhaps *more. (The transfusion complete, Van Helsing begins removing the equipment from them, as — Mina enters, coat on, carrying her traveling bag.)*

MINA. Lucy?! What has happened to her?!

SEWARD.   She's resting now. Professor Van Helsing has completed a transfusion of blood. *(Mina turns to Van Helsing.)* Professor: Lucy's dear friend, Miss Mina Murray.
MINA.   Hello.
VAN HELSING.   An honor. We've done all we can at present.
MINA.   But what of the cause?
VAN HELSING.   A mystery in want of pursuit.
SEWARD.   You've just returned from Budapest?
MINA.   Yes.
SEWARD.   And Mr. Harker, how is he?
MINA.   He is *restored*, God be thanked. His good humor has returned. His terrors have abated. Coming home, it seems, has proved the most soothing medicine. *(Harker enters.)* Ah, here he is. Jonathan, this is Dr. Seward and Professor Van Helsing. They've been looking after — *(As they step toward Harker to greet him, Harker suddenly turns and walks D., away from them — an eerie green light begins to shine on Harker's face. He speaks with an odd, detached terror — as though he were about to go mad.)* Jonathan, what is it?
HARKER.   It is the man himself. *(Seward and Van Helsing look at one another.)* Just now, on the street outside. With mine own two eyes I saw him! My god, it is the man himself!
MINA.   Jonathan, what are you —
HARKER.   But he has *grown young.* The grey hair, the weathered face are gone. Such a change that I thought mine eyes mistaken — but there can be no mistake! It is truly he! Oh, if I had only known! *(Mina rushes to him. The men close in as well, fearing he may come to some harm.)*
MINA.   Enough, now! It's over! You're home and safe —
HARKER.   *(Overlapping.)* And that I, wretched fate, was his solicitor! *(Harker swiftly pulls a very large hunting knife from a sheath on his belt.)* Would I'd had my knife with me then — No! The thought will drive me mad!
MINA.   Jonathan, no!
HARKER.   *I have loosed him on England!* An ever-widening circle of death have I brought to these shores! *(On his knees.)* I had my chance and I did nothing! MY FAILURE SHALL NOT GO UNPUNISHED! *(He quickly braces the knife on the*

ground and is about to <u>impale himself</u> on it, as — Seward and Van Helsing pull him back at the last instant, saving his life. Mina screams, as — Seward and Van Helsing haul Harker out of the room.)

HARKER.	VAN HELSING.
Forgive me! Oh, God, forgive me! Oh, Mina! Mina, forgive me!	Into the other room! Quickly! Prepare a syringe! Morphine — ten milligrams!

(Harker and the men are gone. A low musical drone, as lights pull down and isolate — Mina, as she slumps to the floor, too distraught to cry, too exhausted to move. Then, a sound of wings flapping, as — Mina looks off in the direction which Harker was taken. The sound disappears. Mina looks around. Then ... she walks to her bag and opens it. She removes something from the bag and sits, placing it in front of her ... <u>It is Harker's journal.</u> She looks at it. Then ... she removes the blue ribbon which binds it shut. Sets the ribbon aside, still staring at the closed journal, as — Van Helsing enters.)

VAN HELSING.   He's calmed now. It will — *(He stops when he sees her silence and demeanor. She does not look up at him. Silence.)* Miss Mina?

MINA.   *(Quietly, with resolve.)* A shadowy pall seems to have come over our happiness.

VAN HELSING.   Had I but answers, I would relieve your fears. But, the web is not fully spun — the shape of our misery not yet revealed.

MINA.   We will learn it all too late, I fear. And knowledge is useless to the dead.

VAN HELSING.   Not so, Miss Mina. It is, in fact, on account of the dead that I have come. *(Silence. Mina stares at him ... then lifts the journal.)*

MINA.   I fear some clue lies here within. Jonathan's trust has willed these words remain unread. But, I must know what has brought him to this horrid precipice. *(She looks back to Van Helsing.)* Will you help me, Professor? *(Van Helsing nods, steps in. Mina crosses herself. Then ... she slowly <u>opens the journal</u>, which, simultaneously — <u>Opens a huge door, U.</u> [or: the sound of a huge door opening is heard.] Music. Smoke swirls amid the light, which reveals — Dracula. <u>Much older now.</u> His hair long, grey and wild.*

34

A pallid complexion to his face. Long, yellowed fingernails, danger-ously sharp. He descends [perhaps] a long winding staircase. He speaks in a friendly, gracious manner.)

DRACULA. Welcome to my home! Enter freely and go safely — leaving something of the happiness you bring! *(Harker, car-rying a valise and his briefcase, enters — the castle. Transylvania. This room is defined primarily by a few indeterminate objects which are <u>shrouded in black cloth</u>. An ancient, cob-webbed chandelier hangs above, unlit.)*

HARKER. Count Dracula?

DRACULA. I am Dracula. And I bid you welcome, Mr. Harker. Come in! The night air is chill. You must need eat and rest. *(With a wave of his hand, Dracula makes the candles on the chandelier light up. As Harker looks up at the candles, Dracula takes his bags from him and carries them away.)* The trip is ardu-ous, but the destination worthwhile.

HARKER. I have brought the information you requested re-garding the properties in London. Furthermore, Mr. Dawkins, my superior, recommends that —

DRACULA. *(Politely.)* Mr. Harker.

HARKER. Yes.

DRACULA. You have traveled far. Let your host see to your pleasure before you see to his business. *(Dracula throws back one of the black coverings, revealing — Supper. Set, elegantly, for one. The covered silver platter is <u>identical</u> to the one used by Renfield in the first scene.)* I do hope you're hungry.

HARKER. I am, actually. *(Dracula pulls back Harker's chair. Harker sits.)*

DRACULA. I pray you, sit and sup as you please. You will, I trust, excuse me that I do not join you. I have dined already. *(Dracula prepares to lift the cover of the plate. He stops, looks in Harker's eyes ...)* And I do not sup. *(He uncovers the dish with a flourish. It is a beautiful roast chicken, amid vegetables and sliced fruit.)* Please. Enjoy. *(Harker begins to eat. Dracula blows a cloud of dust from a wine bottle, and looks at the label.)* Ahh. A gift from Attila. The Huns were despicable, but they knew their wine. *(Dracula fills Harker's glass, as — Harker stares at him. Finally, Harker laughs a bit, assuming the remark was in jest.)*

HARKER. *(Jokingly.)* Oh, yes, I see. Passed down, then — from an ancient recipe.

DRACULA. *(Not jokingly.)* A gift. From an ancient adversary. *(Harker looks down at the glass of wine.)*

HARKER. Won't you join me, then?

DRACULA. *(Immediately, indentically.)* Won't you join me, then?

HARKER. Pardon?

DRACULA. My apologies, Mr. Harker — but I must study you. I must learn your ways. *(The wine.)* How is it? *(Dracula gestures for Harker to "drink, please." Harker takes a sip of his wine. Dracula watches him, intently.)*

HARKER. Delicious.

DRACULA. *(Eyeing Harker's neck.)* Yes.

HARKER. You don't partake?

DRACULA. Of *wine*?

HARKER. Yes.

DRACULA. No. Not of wine.

HARKER. If it be not too bold, may I —

DRACULA. *Bold.* Yes! Is that the way of things in London — *bold*? Please — I must know all I can of your city.

HARKER. So, you've never been?

DRACULA. No, but I have my maps and charts. And my books — many books — and as I read, I imagine. And as I imagine, I hunger.

HARKER. London is a fine city.

DRACULA. More to the point, friend: it is a *crowded* city. How I delight in thinking of the bustling streets, peopled with the mad whirl and rush of humanity. Oh, to be in the midst of that banquet of life!

HARKER. I should, I think, enjoy the country. The open spaces. The riding and hunting.

DRACULA. You hunt, do you?

HARKER. When time allows.

DRACULA. And, pray, what do you hunt?

HARKER. Bear, elk, the occasional deer.

DRACULA. Knife or bow?

HARKER. Both, actually.

DRACULA.   I shall like you, Mr. Harker. *(Touching his lips.)* I, too, enjoy the occasional deer. We are fighters, you see. We Carpathians have bravery and conquest in our veins. *(Fiercely, proudly.)* It is no wonder that when the Magyar, the Lombard, the Avar, or the Turk poured his thousands upon our frontier — we drove them back. Legion after legion, they came for our land and we sentenced them to *heaven,* instead. We are a fierce people, Mr. Harker. With a wealth of victories like the Hapsburgs and Romanoffs will never know.

HARKER.   You speak with the passion of one who was there.

DRACULA.   *(Softer, reflective.)* Da Vinci have I known. Charlemagne. Bach. *(Harker looks at him, says nothing.)* But, great men, like galaxies, end as dust. We Carpathians have come to know that the early times, the warlike days are over. In our world, Mr. Harker, blood is too precious a thing to be spilt. *(A cock crows, in the distance. Dracula rises.)* But, I have spoken too long. It is near morning and I must retire. I leave you, then, to your rest. *(He throws back another black covering, revealing — a small bed, and night table. On the bed, inexplicably, is Harker's valise and briefcase which we saw Dracula carry off, elsewhere. On the table is a pitcher and basin of water, and a towel.)* One thing, Mr. Harker: You may go anywhere you like in the castle, except where the doors are locked, where of course you will not wish to go. We are in Transylvania; and Transylvania is not England. Our ways are not your ways, and there shall be to you many strange things. But, did you see with my eyes … and know with my knowledge … you would better understand. *(Cock crows, again.)* Good night, then. And good morning. *(With a sweeping flourish of his cape, he turns and goes, as lights isolate — Harker, standing by the night stand, removing his shirt, and — Mina, holding the journal, with Van Helsing near her. Mina begins to close the journal.)*

VAN HELSING.   Miss Mina — read on.

MINA.   I'm afraid I'm mistaken, Professor. There is nothing here to enlighten us. *(Van Helsing takes her hand — stopping her from closing the journal.)*

VAN HELSING.   Miss Mina, I beg of you. These notes — this shorthand — was written for a reason. We must read on!

MINA. I've not time to waste. These are travel notes — business dealings with an aging nobleman — nothing more. The secrets Jonathan spoke of must be elsewhere, they must —
VAN HELSING. *(His face very close to hers.)* Listen to me: Hidden in the world — in the dark creases of books, in the swirl of ink on innocent pages — hidden there are wild and mysterious things. And if we are to reach into the darkness and bring Jonathan a gleam of peace — we must not be deterred. We must, from this moment on, be relentless. WE MUST KNOW THE ALL OF IT. *(Silence. Mina stares at him. He puts the open journal back into her hands.)* Now: page forward, Miss Mina. I pray you: page forward and read on. *(Mina pages forward in the journal, as — Harker stands in his undershirt. He holds the rosary in his hand ... looks at it ... then puts it around his neck. He has retrieved a mug of shaving creme and a straight razor from his bag. He applies a small amount of creme to one side of his neck, preparing to shave. Sound of a wolf howling, long and plaintive. Harker lifts a small mirror, holds it up in front of him. Another wolf howls. Harker lifts the razor and is about to bring the razor to his neck, when — Dracula appears, behind him. He watches Harker from a distance, "mirroring" Harker's motions delicately, with his fingers, as — Harker shaves. <u>He cannot, of course, see Dracula in the mirror</u>. Still another wolf howls, followed by — a slight, delicious sigh from Dracula, his eyes closed, savoring the touch, the memory ... Harker, hearing the sigh, asks:)*
HARKER. Who's there? *(Startled, Harker, looks quickly into the mirror. He angles the mirror in several ways, trying to find Dracula's image in it — <u>without success</u>. Harker begins to turn:)*
DRACULA. You needn't turn. I don't wish to disturb you. *(Strangely, nervously, Harker continues shaving.)* Only to study you. To learn the curve of your neck.
HARKER. I will be leaving in the morning. I had not intended to stay a full week. And, since, our business is nearly complete, I shall —
DRACULA. Mr. Harker —
HARKER. Yes?
DRACULA. You've cut yourself. *(Harker sees it in the mirror.)*
HARKER. So, I have. *(Harker begins to reach for the towel.)*

DRACULA. Please. Allow me. *(Wolf howls, as — Dracula approaches, until he is directly behind Harker. He takes the towel from Harker. With one hand, Dracula gently tilts Harker's head to one side, exposing his neck, exposing the cut. A loud wolf howl, as — Dracula throws back his head, saying:)* Ah, the Children of the Night. What beautiful music they make! *(Dracula opens his mouth, revealing the <u>long, canine teeth</u> for the first time. With his other hand, he lets the towel fall to the ground. <u>As he is about to plunge his teeth into Harker's neck</u> — The piercing sound of a huge door slamming shut is heard. Harker turns, shocked by the sound, and — <u>seeing the crucifix</u>, Dracula lets go of Harker and stumbles back, away, with a scream — more wolves howling. More music. Harker takes hold of the crucifix and looks down at it, looks up at Dracula, frightened, confused.)* You must take care, Mr. Harker! Take care how you cut yourself — it is more dangerous than you think in this country!

HARKER. *(Grabbing the towel from the floor.)* Where are my papers? *(Dracula stares at him.)* Answer me, please! All my papers — they're gone — everything — my notes, letters, even the *deed to the property itself* — as yet unsigned — gone —

DRACULA. You've been blessed with a disappearance! How fortunate!

MINA. But this journal, how did it survive?

VAN HELSING. The *shorthand* — he knew not its contents!

HARKER. And my clothes — all but what I have on is missing!

DRACULA. I'll find you a nice cape. Now, tell me of my new home.

HARKER. I've told you. For a week now, I've —

DRACULA. Tell me again — I must be certain. Is it an old place?

HARKER. Yes, of course, as I've told you each night, it was formerly a —

DRACULA. I'm so glad. For you see, Mr. Harker, I am old — old in ways which few can rival or understand — and to live in a new house would kill me. Do tell me the name again. *(A high ringing sound, as — Dracula <u>extends his fingers</u> toward Harker's head. Harker leans forward a bit, staring at Dracula, fro-*

zen, saying nothing. The sound of digging begins softly, distantly.) Excellent! A fine and noble name! And, it's location? *(Again, Dracula extends his fingers, and, again, Harker stares at Dracula, saying nothing.)* Splendid!

VAN HELSING.   Wait, go back! We must know! *(Mina turns the page back.)* The name and location — we must know it!

MINA.   *(Looking in the book.)* It's not here — there is nothing here —

VAN HELSING.   *(Grabbing the book.)* Let me see that!

MINA.   The page is burned away — burned away in two places —

VAN HELSING.   How can that be? *(The sound of digging is now much louder.)*

DRACULA.   And as for *light,* tell me — is it well appointed?

HARKER.   *(Bitterly.)* Well — no — in fact, it is quite shrouded in darkness —

DRACULA.   I commend you, Mr. Harker. I love the shade and the shadow; the solitude and potent quiet of the night.

HARKER.   *(Agitated.)* But there is no quiet here, only this digging! I am forever hearing the sound. Shovels digging, doors being opened and shut —

DRACULA.   Only the gypsies below, doing my bidding.

HARKER.   And the boxes? Large boxes being hauled out — the last three days and nights — what is the meaning of that?

DRACULA.   That work is entrusted to another solicitor, my friend. *(A threat.)* I beg you not to press me further. *I must go to England.* I am *starving* here. For want of companionship. For want of life! *(Dracula removes a paper — the deed — from his clothing.)* Here is the deed. It lacks only your signature.

HARKER.   How did you —

DRACULA.   *(He produces a writing instrument. He holds it out to Harker, who stares at it, not moving. Sound of bats shrieking joins the howl of the wolves, and the music.)* Come, Mr Harker. Finish what you started. *(Another long moment of standoff, then, finally — Harker grabs the writing instrument and signs the deed. Dracula smiles.)* Your good work shall be rewarded ten-fold.

HARKER.   I want to leave.

DRACULA.   Very well.

HARKER. I want to leave *tonight*.

DRACULA. I'm afraid that's impossible.

HARKER. Why?

DRACULA. My coachman and horses are away.

HARKER. I'll walk!

DRACULA. Alone among the wolves?!

HARKER. I'll hazard a chance. Now, please, point me to the door!

DRACULA. Oh, Mr. Harker, I'll point you to ALL the doors! *(Dracula gestures with a flourish, producing — a deafening cacophony of doors being bolted shut. Dracula laughs heartily over this sound.)*

HARKER. *(Overlapping the sound of the doors.)* Wait! No!

MINA. *(Overlapping Harker.)* JONATHAN!

DRACULA. You English have a phrase: "Welcome the coming, speed the parting guest!" You see, I am happy, Mr. Harker, to speed your parting — *(And, saying this, he extends his fingers towards Harker's eyes, freezing him in his tracks. Harker fights to stay conscious — holding his own head with his hands — but — Dracula gradually hypnotizes him during the following speech ... until Harker is lying on the bed, immobile.)*

HARKER. *(Fighting the hypnosis.)* No — let me go — I must go —

DRACULA. I have all I need of you, Mr. Harker. Your work is at an end.

HARKER. *(Weakening.)* I must tell them — tell them of the digging — the boxes of earth —

DRACULA. And, I shall carry your memory with me to England.

HARKER. *(Barely audible.)* Mina — Mina, be warned — oh, Mina ... *(The hypnosis complete, Harker lies on the bed. With another gesture, Dracula snuffs the candles on the chandelier out. He turns and goes, as lights isolate — the bed. It is lit by a shaft of moonlight. Light also remains on Mina and Van Helsing.)*

VAN HELSING. That is enough for tonight! Put yourself through no more, I beg of you —

MINA. No, you're right, Professor — I must page forward, I must know it, I must know it all! *(Mina flips quickly through more pages. As she does, there is — motion on the bed, all around*

41

Harker. Motion under the sheets, then arms ... and legs ... coming up out of the bed [or: from under and behind the bed.] Sound of passionate breathing, hissing, sinister whispers, the pounding of a heart, growing faster and faster, as — the arms and legs slither around on Harker's body, slowly waking him, seductively, erotically — then, their faces emerge ... they are the two vixens we glimpsed earlier. White faces, blood-red mouths, wild hair, flowing garments ... and, of course, fanged teeth. Sound builds. Harker responds, still half-asleep, caressing the vixens, letting himself be kissed on the mouth, kissed all over his body, pleasurably. Then ... his expression begins to change. He wakes fully and sees their fanged-teeth, their red eyes. He realizes his arms and legs are tied to the bed. He realizes he is in mortal danger.)

HARKER. What are you?! NO! LET ME GO! *(The Vixens hover just above his exposed neck on either side. They look at each other, lick their lips, smile, and then:)*

HARKER.	MINA.
AHHHHHHHH!!!!!	NOOOOOOOOO!!!!!

(They plunge their teeth towards his neck, as — Dracula instantly appears, holding a small cloth sack, screaming volcanically.)

DRACULA. HOW DARE YOU! HOW DARE YOU TOUCH HIM! HE IS *MINE!!!* *(The Vixens are thrown aside by Dracula's gesture. They crawl about on the ground — furious, helpless, breathing wildly.)* Back, both of you! Back to your place! Your time with him will come! Tomorrow I set sail, and then he shall be yours. *(The Vixens coo, moan and lick their lips.)* You may feast upon him then at your will.

VIXEN ONE. And tonight?

DRACULA. What of it?

VIXEN TWO. Are we to have nothing tonight? *(From the cloth bag, he pulls a tiny, crying baby, holding it by the legs. The Vixens eyes light up, hungrily. Harker looks on, horrified.)*

VAN HELSING. My god! *(Dracula quickly puts the baby back into the cloth bag — and hands the bag to the Vixens. They take the bag — reaching into it, cooing and whispering and touching the [unseen] baby lovingly. They stand behind the bed — directly over Harker's head. Music and sounds build, as — Dracula throws back one final black covering, revealing — a wooden box, coffin-sized, iden-*

tical to the one seen earlier. Dracula opens the box and steps inside, saying:)

DRACULA.   And so, my great good thanks to you, Mr. Harker! I shall leave you in the good hands of the loving Carpathian people! *(The Vixens plunge their faces down into the bag as they <u>devour the baby</u>. The <u>blood drips out of the bag and falls onto Harker's face and chest</u>, below them. The Vixens are ravenous, sloppy eaters — their faces growing red and wet with the fertile pleasures of fresh life. Dracula <u>climbs into the wooden box</u>, as — Mina drops the journal and runs to the edge of the stage, C., throwing herself to the ground — Van Helsing stands, holding the journal — Renfield, caged [or: in a shaft of light], appears.)*

MINA.	HARKER.	RENFIELD.
JONATHAN!!!	NOOOOOO!!!	MASTER!!!

DRACULA.   AND I, MR. HARKER —

RENFIELD.   I'M HERE MASTER!!!

VAN HELSING.   MY GOD, IT'S TRUE!

DRACULA.   — I AM BOUND FOR ENGLAND!!! *(Music very quickly crescendos, as — the Vixens eat — Harker screams — Mina sobs — Renfield rants — Van Helsing prays aloud to the heavens, crossing himself — And, Dracula <u>lowers himself into the box</u>, and then <u>closes the lid of the box, slamming it shut</u> — instant <u>silence</u>. All lights <u>out</u>, except for a shaft of light on — Mina. Still crying, quietly, she raises her head. Next to her, on the ground, its head [perhaps] moving ever-so-slightly, is — a large black raven. Mina stares at the raven, wiping her tears. She reaches out her hand, fearfully at first, toward the raven's head. She gently touches the raven's head with her fingers, as — final quick burst of music, loud. Light on Mina snaps out, fast.)*

END OF ACT ONE

ACT TWO

A guest room at the asylum. Comfortably appointed, but ob-
viously concerned with security — bars on the window, etc.
A bed, the window, and a small table and chairs are essen-
tial. Black drapes — similar to those in Lucy's room in Act
One — frame the window.

Van Helsing and Seward are busily festooning the entire room
with strings of garlic, rubbing the window panes and cur-
tains, draping the bed.

VAN HELSING. The outer gate, as you say, is guarded at
all times?
SEWARD. Yes.
VAN HELSING. And there is no other access to this room?
SEWARD. None, whatsoever. The room was built for digni-
taries who, on occasion, would visit the asylum — to show they
were a "friend to those less fortunate." Most quickly found they
could not stomach the inmates — and thus spent their time
safely locked away in here. *(Van Helsing nods, approvingly, and*
then sees something on the floor in the center of the room. He kneels
and looks at it.) What is it?
VAN HELSING. Just a bit of dirt.
SEWARD. I'll have the staff be more thorough.
VAN HELSING. See, too, that they allow no strangers to
enter.
SEWARD. They won't, I assure you.
VAN HELSING. Assurance is not enough, John. They must
be vigilant. They must be rigorously on-guard against the unknown. *(He returns to his work in the room.)* Pay special atten-
tion to the doors and windows.
SEWARD. Professor, I'm afraid I don't understand —
VAN HELSING. It was necessary to move Lucy from her

home to a safer room. You have provided that, here at the asylum.

SEWARD.   But, safe from *what*?

VAN HELSING.   Do not fear, John, to think the most unprobable. And, as you think it, remember our promise to one another: to not enlighten, and thus, not *alarm*, the others. There is misery enough among them.

SEWARD.   But what effect will garlic have on her loss of blood?

VAN. HELSING.   Perhaps none. And perhaps all. *(Van Helsing stops in his work and turns to Seward.)* You have been of great help to her, John. And, in no less than blood, she is your bride.

SEWARD.   No man knows — till he experiences it — what it is to feel his own life drawn away and into the veins of the woman he adores.

VAN HELSING.   Further, I trust in your inspection you encountered the marks on Miss Lucy's neck.

SEWARD.   Yes. I did.

VAN HELSING.   And you mean to tell me you have no suspicion as to what is killing your dear Lucy?

SEWARD.   A nervous prostration following on great loss of blood.

VAN HELSING.   And how was the blood lost? *(Seward stares at him.)* John, it is the fault of our science that it wants to explain everything — and if it fails, then it says there is nothing to explain.

SEWARD.   But if her blood — great quantities of her blood — was lost through a wound in her neck, *where did it go?* It was not on her clothing, her bedding, it was nowhere to be seen. If it happened as you say: *what took it out?* (Mina enters, carrying a large box wrapped with a colorful ribbon.)

MINA.   A package has arrived for you, Professor.

VAN HELSING.   Splendid. If you'll place it on the bed. *(She does.)* And Miss Lucy?

MINA.   She's on her way.

SEWARD.   I'll see her up. Excuse me. *(Seward exits.)*

MINA.   Professor Van Helsing, I must ask —

VAN HELSING.   Oh, Miss Mina, how can I say what I owe
to you? Mr. Harker's journal was as sunshine to me. It opened
a gate shrouded in superstition and disregard — and it dazzled
me with insight.

MINA.   Yes, I gather that, but even still —

VAN HELSING.   If ever Abraham Van Helsing can do anything for you or yours, if ever I may serve you as a friend, I
trust you will let me know. There are darknesses in this life,
and there are lights; and you, Miss Mina, are surely one of
the lights.

MINA.   *(Pause.)* There is something.

VAN HELSING.   Please.

MINA.   Lucy has told you of her dreams. But, I fear they
are not dreams.

VAN HELSING.   What do you mean?

MINA.   Many nights I would wake to find her gone. Walk-
ing in her sleep, toward the cliffs. Many nights I found her
there and brought her home. Then, she began to grow ill.
(Pause.) Professor, I have pledged her my confidence, so I must
ask you —

VAN HELSING.   Miss Mina, your words have my trust. Now,
when you found her at the cliffs, was she alone?

MINA.   Yes. Each time but one. *(Van Helsing sits, curious.)*
Once there was a man — or a shadow of a man — all in black,
his face in shadow. I thought nothing of it till reading
Jonathan's journal. The man he described, and what he wrote
of the Count's plans to come to London — I know not what
this means, but there seems to be some thread of continuity,
some — *(Stops.)* No, it is too strange. You will laugh and think
me foolish.

VAN HELSING.   Oh, my dear, I have learned not to belittle
anyone's beliefs — no matter how strange — for it is not the
ordinary things which close our minds — but the *extraordinary
things,* those mysteries on the fringe of our thinking.

MINA.   This, then, my request: I want to know what
you know. I want to be informed of what you learn, as you
learn it.

VAN HELSING.   *(Pause.)* Miss Mina, while it is true that Mr.

Harker's suffering falls within the range of my experience —

MINA. You have promised your friendship. Is your promise a worthy one or not? *(Lucy enters, ushered in by Seward. She remains extremely pale.)*

SEWARD. Here we are.

LUCY. It's just as you described.

MINA. *Professor?*

VAN HELSING. You have my word.

LUCY. But you said nothing of the smell. My God!

VAN HELSING. A medicinal contrivance, nothing more.

SEWARD. One of us will stay here with you at all times — to keep watch, to assure your safety. *(Van Helsing hands her the wrapped box.)*

VAN HELSING. And this, Miss Lucy, is for you.

LUCY. Such flattery do the unwell receive! *(She opens the box. Removes a beautiful wreath of garlic.)* Oh, Professor, such a beautiful wreath. I shall hang it on the —

VAN HELSING. It's to be worn.

LUCY. *Worn? (He places the wreath over her head.)*

VAN HELSING. Like this.

LUCY. Well, the garlic around the window is one thing, sir. But, I'm afraid I can't — *(She begins to remove the wreath. Van Helsing, with a firm hand, stops her.)*

VAN HELSING. It will guard against your bad dreams, Miss Lucy —

LUCY. *(With a laugh.)* But, it's common garlic! I fear you're having a joke on me, Professor —

VAN HELSING. *(Fervently.)* I warn you: do not thwart me! There is no jest in what I do! *(They all look at him, stunned by his outburst.)* Only grim purpose. Take care to mind me, if not for your own sake, then for that of the others. *(Lucy stares at him, curious. Then she lowers the wreath back down around her neck.)*

LUCY. I trust you have reasons for what you do, but I must say it puzzles me. *(With a laugh.)* Were a stranger to walk in, they'd think you were working a spell to keep out an evil spirit!

VAN HELSING. *(Simply.)* Maybe I am. *(An Attendant rushes in to the room.)*

ATTENDANT. Dr. Seward!

SEWARD. What is it?

ATTENDANT. It's Renfield — you must come! *(Seward leaves Lucy's side and starts out.)*

LUCY. John —

VAN HELSING. *(To Seward, urgently.)* May I come with you? This madman may serve as an index for our investigation.

SEWARD. In what way?

VAN HELSING. Have not his outbursts coincided with Lucy's bad dreams? *(Seward stares at him, as Van Helsing turns quickly to Lucy.)* We leave you in the best of hands. *(Van Helsing rushes off. Seward follows.)*

LUCY. Professor — *(Pause, turns to Mina.)* What is happening to me?

MINA. You musn't think of it. You need only to rest and —

LUCY. Mina, promise me this.

MINA. Anything at all.

LUCY. Promise you'll forgive me.

MINA. Lucy, don't be silly — forgive you for what?

LUCY. For something I know not of. But there are dark imaginings in me. I have fought to rid my mind of them ... but they rise up within me, bringing color to my cheeks and a sickly taste in my mouth. *(Mina stares at her.)* God help me, Mina. I don't know what I've become. *(Lights shift quickly to — Renfield's cell. Renfield sits, inexplicably, in a small, odd, ornate chair. It seems to be made of golden bones, bedecked with jewels. He sits, unchained, in a distinguished manner, smoking an imaginary cigarette, holding court with great élan. As Renfield talks, Seward and Van Helsing rush in. An Attendant is outside the cell.)*

RENFIELD. Oh, and do let me recount how she came into the room: With such *joie de vivre*, such an easy gracefulness which would command the respect of any lunatic — for easiness is the one quality mad people respect the most. *(Seeing the men.)* Arrive–ed from Gloucester! Pray, what news?

SEWARD. *(To the Attendant.)* What is — where did this chair come from? *(The Attendant gestures that "he has no idea," as:)*

RENFIELD. From one who holds me in high esteem.

VAN HELSING. From the one you call Master?

RENFIELD. *(To Seward, referring to Van Helsing.)* Oh, where *did* you find him?

SEWARD. Renfield, listen to me —

RENFIELD. And the girl, John! Oh, no *wonder* you're heart-broken. She came by, using an assumed name. I found that dashing. We talked. I spoke of my fondness for Mozart — but she bested me with her treatise on Bach.

SEWARD. Miss Lucy has been upstairs all day —

RENFIELD. She's a very clever girl! She called herself *Mina*, claimed to be lost — but then, we're all lost in here, aren't we? I do hope she found her way.

VAN HELSING. You're speaking of Miss Mina, then?

RENFIELD. Name them what you will, right, Johnny? Any bride will do.

SEWARD. *(Furious.)* I will not tolerate this kind of —

VAN HELSING. John! Match not madness with wits. Pursue it as it plays.

RENFIELD. Her voice, like water: "Could you point me to the guest room, I seem to have taken a wrong turn." I quoth her a sonnet and sent her on her way. A lovely creature. She shall be missed.

VAN HELSING. Missed? Do say more. In what way will she be missed? *(Renfield carefully drops his imaginary cigarette to the ground and puts it out with his foot. He leans forward, speaks with an urgent clarity.)*

RENFIELD. I entreat you, Dr. Seward, to let me out of this madhouse. Send me away from here — anywhere you will — or I will be forced to do something terrible.

VAN HELSING. And what would that be?

RENFIELD. I am in great danger, sir!

SEWARD. You're in no danger at all. You're perfectly safe here —

RENFIELD. I am speaking from the depth of my soul. I beg of you. You don't know what you do by keeping me here! You don't know whom you shall harm — and I, bound to secrecy, cannot tell you!

SEWARD. *(Angrily.)* You will stay here till the court deems you fit, and these wild harangues in no way further your wish to be considered sane! *(And now, a total change in Renfield. He stands on the chair, leaps at the men, leaps about the cell with abandon. This is not dementia — but a fierce, purposeful fury. The Men shout ad-libs, trying to calm him, make sense of him.)*

RENFIELD.   Send me where you will! Bind me! Beat me! Drag me away! Tie me to a rock and throw me in a jail — do whatever you must, BUT TAKE ME FROM HERE AND SAVE MY SOUL FROM GUILT!

VAN HELSING.	SEWARD.
What guilt do you speak of?	Calm yourself and explain —

RENFIELD.   Oh — hear me — by all you hold sacred — by all you hold dear — by your love that is lost — by your hope that still lives — for the sake of the dear God Almighty —

SEWARD.	VAN HELSING.
THAT'S ENOUGH NOW —	Hear him out —

RENFIELD.   DON'T YOU SEE, JOHNNY, I AM *CURED!* I AM NO LUNATIC IN A MAD FIT — BUT A SANE MAN FIGHTING FOR HIS SOUL!

SEWARD.   *(To the Attendant.)* See that he goes nowhere. *(In a flash of rage, Renfield produces a small, curved <u>sword</u>. [It is perhaps part of the chair.] He takes a wild swing at Seward, cutting him on the arm.)*

RENFIELD.   HEAR ME NOW! *(Seward grabs his cut arm, as his shirt begins to bloody. The Attendant rushes out. Renfield's attention shifts instantly to the sword. He kneels, staring at the blood on the sword. Then, he begins to <u>lick the blood from the sword</u>. This calms and delights him. He speaks, softly, repeatedly, to himself:)* The blood is the life ... the blood is the life ... the blood is the life ...

SEWARD.   *(Bitterly, overlapping Renfield.)* And what now? What is your thesis now?

VAN HELSING.   My thesis is this: I want you to believe.

SEWARD.   To believe what?!

VAN HELSING.   *To believe in things that you cannot.* That is essence of faith. To accept the things which cannot be proved!

SEWARD.   With all due respect, my patience with your cryptic homilies is coming to an end. *(Van Helsing grabs Seward, forcefully and urgently.)*

VAN HELSING. Can you tell me why men — in all ages and all places — have believed that there are some few who *live on always?* That there are men and women who *cannot die?*
RENFIELD. *(Looking up at them, suddenly, cogently.)* I did what I could to warn you. Remember that. *(They look at Renfield, as lights shift to — the guest room at the Asylum. Sunset. The final crescent of a huge sun is seen outside the window. During the following, it will* set completely, *slowly disappearing from view. Lucy is in bed, asleep. She wears the wreath of garlic around her neck. Her color, however, is* restored. *She looks much like she did at the beginning of the play — beautiful, tranquil. Mina sits in a chair near the bed, also asleep, Harker's journal open on her lap. Faintly, in the distance, a boys' choir sings a solemn, beautiful hymn. A Female Attendant enters, carrying tea on a tray. Waking neither of the women, she sets the tray in the room ... then begins to leave. She stops. She sees something. She walks D. ... bends down to inspect something on the floor in the center of the room. Shrugs, slightly. From her apron, she removes a small hand-broom. She sweeps a small bit of dirt from the rug — and into her open hand. Finished with this task, she starts to leave, as — Seward enters the room. His arm is bandaged. He whispers to the Female Attendant.)*
SEWARD. How is she?
FEMALE ATTENDANT. I don't know, Doctor. Miss Mina's been with her. *(Seward nods. The Female Attendant exits. Seward sees the tea tray. He goes to it, begins to pour a cup of tea, then — Stops. His eyes have caught sight of — Lucy. In her sleep, she is* removing the wreath of garlic *from around her neck. Never waking, Lucy tosses the wreath aside, then lies back and sleeps, peacefully. Seward stands, frozen, watching her, as — Mina wakes.)*
MINA. Doctor?
SEWARD. *(Startled.)* What —
MINA. What is it? *(Seeing his bandaged arm.)* What has happened to your arm?
SEWARD. Oh — clumsiness, I'm afraid. Miss Mina, if I may — *(Pause, she looks up at him, she nods.)* Did you have occasion to see one of my patients earlier today?
MINA. In fact, I did. I became lost, entered a corridor opened a large door, and found myself in the midst of your

inmates. I was quite flummoxed. I spoke to a Count Renfield.

SEWARD. Count?

MINA. Or so he called himself. He told me of his love for the violin. *(Seward stares at her as she moves away.)* Well, I'll leave our dear Lucy to you. She seems much better. Her sleep is very peaceful. Her color restored.

SEWARD. And Mr. Harker, how is he?

MINA. Professor Van Helsing has met with him. And with good results, I think. *(Takes his hand.)* May God's kindness be with us all. *(Mina goes. Seward looks back at Lucy. He picks up the wreath from wherever Lucy threw it. Looks at it. Carries it to the bed. He turns Lucy's head a bit, planning to replace the wreath around her neck. He pulls back her hair — giving him a view of her neck. He stops. He drops the wreath. He looks more closely at her neck. Touches her neck, gently, with his fingers. He backs away from the bed ... surprised, overjoyed. He moves quickly to the entrance and yells off.)*

SEWARD. Miss, come quickly! *(He looks back at Lucy, who is still sleeping, as — the Female Attendant rushes in. Seward takes hold of her, urgently.)* Find Professor Van Helsing. Send him directly here. *(The Female Attendant nods.)* Tell him they are gone! The marks on her neck — they have *disappeared!* She is *healed!* Quickly now — go! *(The Female Attendant nods and rushes off. Seward returns to the bed, joyously, and takes Lucy's hand. She does not wake. The huge sun has now completely set. Silence. Seward's expression changes. He squeezes her hand, several times ... then slaps it, again and again.)* Lucy. *(He feels her pulse, touches her forehead.)* Lucy, wake up. Lucy, please. Lucy, come on now — wake up — *(He lifts her eye lids, he begins to shake her.)* Lucy! Oh, my god — Lucy ... *(He takes her hand mirror and holds it near her mouth and nose. Looks at the mirror. Nothing. He slowly closes her eyes. He crosses himself. He drops to his knees next to the bed, putting his head on her stomach. He cries, softly.)* No ... please, god ... no ... *(A long moment of nothing but Seward's soft, aching cries. Then, unseen by Seward — Lucy's eyes open. She watches him cry, his head still on her stomach.)*

LUCY. *(Softly, sweetly.)* Oh, Johnny, don't cry. *(Music, as — Seward opens his eyes wide, stares front, does not move.)* I'm right

here. I'm right here with you. *(He lifts his head slowly, and, seeing her open eyes — he jumps back, away.)*
SEWARD. Lucy?
LUCY. We're all alone, Johnny.
SEWARD. Lucy, it can't be.
LUCY. Come here. *(He does not move.)* Please. *(He stares at her. Then, he approaches, tentatively. Still keeping some distance, he takes hold of her wrist and feels her pulse.)* Such warm hands. I like that.
SEWARD. You've no pulse, Lucy. No pulse at all. Lucy, what is —
LUCY. Kiss me. *(He drops her arm, stands there, frozen.)* Please, Johnny. Haven't you wanted to? *I* have. *(He continues to stare at her. She is up now, kneeling on the bed, leaning toward him. Sweetly, alluring.)* Oh, my love, I'm so glad you're here. Please … kiss me. *(She reaches out her arms to him.)* I broke your heart, Johnny. And I shall never rest till you forgive me. Please … take me back. Let me show you my true heart. *(He steps toward her, and sits on the edge of the bed. She takes him gently in her arms — and holds his head lovingly to her chest. She strokes his hair, speaks softly.)* That's it. That's it. Oh, I've wanted this for so long. *(He nods, holding her more tightly, his head still tight against her chest.)* You were right, you know. We do, each of us, have a secret life. *(She bares her teeth, fully — revealing huge, hideous fangs, but still speaks sweetly, seductively. He, of course, has not yet seen her face.)* And I want you to know mine. So, please, Johnny … close your eyes. Will you do that for me? *(He nods. He closes his eyes. He pulls his head away from her chest. She licks her lips, hungrily.)* Good. Now … kiss me. *(She is breathing heavily now, her fangs bared — He leans forward, slowly, eyes still closed, to kiss her — Her mouth moves toward his neck, her teeth are about to pierce his flesh, as — Van Helsing rushes in, followed by Harker. Van Helsing tackles Seward — pulling him out of Lucy's grasp.)*
VAN HELSING. NOT FOR YOUR LIFE! *(Lucy stands on the bed, in a rage, hissing and gasping, clawing and shrieking — Seward lands on the floor, opposite — Van Helsing stands between them, as Harker looks on.)* NOT FOR YOUR LIVING SOUL OR MINE — YOU SHALL NOT HAVE HIM! *(Seward has now clearly seen*

this hideous version of Lucy for the first time.)

SEWARD.   My god — what has happened to her?! *(Lucy be-gins to leap down from the bed onto Van Helsing.)*

LUCY.   BE MINE! (— *just as Van Helsing produces a large cru-cifix.)*

VAN HELSING.   NEVER! *(The crucifix stops her — she writhes, hideously — as though on fire — caught in the throes of a vicious spasm ... then ... drops down onto the bed ... exhausted ... crying softly.... Van Helsing moves closer to her. Harker helps Seward to his feet, as they both watch Lucy.)*

SEWARD.   What in god's name has —

VAN HELSING.   Quiet, John. It is leaving her. *(Lucy raises her head, slowly, eyes closed — a sad, beautiful look on her face. She slowly opens her eyes. The rage has now left her completely. She is herself, once again.)*

LUCY.   My true friend ... *(Looking at Seward, speaking to Van Helsing.)* ... guard him from me and give me peace ... keep him safe, for he is my true friend!

VAN HELSING.   I swear on it. *(Lucy slumps quietly down onto the bed. She does not move. Long silence. A bell tolls, mournfully, in the distance. Seward turns to Van Helsing.)* That's all, now. She's gone from us. *(Silence. Seward looks down at Lucy's body.)*

SEWARD.   *(Softly.)* God be thanked, her suffering is at an end.

VAN HELSING.   Not so, John. I'm afraid this is only the be-ginning. *(The men both look at him.)* We must arrange for the entombment as soon as possible. Then, we must wait.

HARKER.   Wait for what?

VAN HELSING.   There are strange and terrible days ahead of us. I entreat you: have faith in me. And, if it be in your heart: pity me.

SEWARD.   For what reason? It is I who've lost the light of my life.

VAN HELSING.   Pity me because *I know why.*

SEWARD.   But you tell us nothing! You test the limits of my sympathetic understanding.

VAN HELSING.   *(Approaching Harker.)* Now, Mr. Harker, from the facts of your journal: you are in no danger. Nor is Miss Mina. This room, in fact — all of the asylum, will remain safe *so long as no stranger is granted permission to enter.* You were right, Mr. Harker: the Count is somewhere in London, and we shall find his whereabouts through you.

HARKER.   The name of the property, though, remains lost to me.

VAN HELSING.   As he burned it from your journal, so, too, he burned it from your mind.

HARKER.   I will find it, Professor! I am in your debt. You've shown me that I *did* see what I imagined — and, for that cure, I am ever at your service. *(They shake hands.)*

VAN HELSING.   Let us then be friends for all our lives. *(Van Helsing now turns to Seward who remains at Lucy's bedside.)* Now, there is bitter water we must pass through, John, before we arrive at the sweet.

SEWARD.   ENOUGH. Either tell me your plan or leave us in peace. I'm through being spoken to as though I were a child.

VAN HELSING.   You are a grown man, is that right?

SEWARD.   That's right.

VAN HELSING.   And no longer my student.

SEWARD.   That's right.

VAN HELSING.   And the man who once saved my life.

SEWARD.   Yes.

VAN HELSING.   Well, John, our accounts are settled.

SEWARD.   What does that mean?

VAN HELSING.   I have just saved yours. *(Seward stares at him.)* She is the Un-Dead. The restless blood-letting *vampir.* She has been cursed with immortality and must go on — age after age — preying on the life-blood of humanity, and multiplying the evils of the world in an ever-widening circle of malevolent destruction! *Nosferatu!* Scourge of Christendom, the Lords of Lucifer!

SEWARD.   Professor, have you gone mad?!

VAN HELSING.   Oh, that I had! Madness would be easy to bear compared with a truth such as this. Why, friend, do you think I've taken such time, such care to tell you? Knowing of your love for her, I wished to be gentle — but it is no longer your heart which is at risk, John ... but your heart's *emission.*

55

SEWARD.   If this wild account be so, we are too late — is that right? Her soul is already lost —

VAN HELSING.   Lost, but for our daring. Following her burial, we shall go to her tomb — this in secret to protect her good name, and to bring no more of her kind down upon us — and, once there ... *we shall drive a stake through her heart and sever her head from her body.*

HARKER.   Professor —!

SEWARD.   *(Overlapping.)* What have I done that you would torture me so?! I will never consent to that. I will not have her too-young grave dishonored in such a way. It's unthinkable, that you, a learned man, would —

VAN HELSING.   No, John. *I'll show you the unthinkable.* If you dare join me at her tomb, the night of her burial, I will convince you of my plan. *(Seward stares at him, as lights shift to — Renfield's cell. Renfield sits in a tight ball on the ground. The chair is gone. An Attendant enters, and sets a large, steaming cup of liquid in the cell, near him.)*

ATTENDANT.   Drink up, now. That's a good boy. *(The Attendant leaves. Renfield stares at the cup. The steam pours over the sides of the cup like fog. Then, from out of nowhere, the amplified voice of Dracula is heard.)*

VOICE OF DRACULA.   Won't you ask me to enter? *(Renfield looks, frantically, around the room.)* My patience is wearing thin.

RENFIELD.   Where are you?

VOICE OF DRACULA.   I am everywhere. I am rock and water, cloud and fog. I am the hunt in the eyes of the beasts.

RENFIELD.   I've told you before — *(He suddenly looks down at the steam pouring from the cup. He kneels and speaks, cautiously, to the steam.)* I've told you "No." I will not be damned as the devil's accomplice.

VOICE OF DRACULA.   Did I not send you the *flies?* Great, fat ones with steel and sapphire on their wings. And then, the *moths* — with the heads of Death emblazoned on their backs?

RENFIELD.   *(Now rocking back and forth.)* The *Acherontia atropos!*

VOICE OF DRACULA.   Yes! But I will not stop there.

RENFIELD.   *(Covering his ears.)* No more — I am listening

no more —

VOICE OF DRACULA. *Rats. (Renfield gradually uncovers his ears, and stands. Music, as — the light in the cell gradually becomes fully blood red.)* Rats, rats and more rats! Hundreds, thousands, millions of them. And *every one a life!*

RENFIELD. No!

VOICE OF DRACULA. And CATS to eat the rats. And DOGS to eat the cats. All filled with luscious red blood — all filled with years and years of *LIFE!*

RENFIELD. *(Feverishly now.)* And the DOGS? What to eat the DOGS?! *(The piercing sound of a whip striking flesh.)*

VOICE OF DRACULA. *(His voice echoing through the cell.)* THE WOLVES! *(Wolves howl, as the red light in the room pulses.)*

RENFIELD. *(Licking his lips, tearing at his clothing.)* Aaahhhhh!

VOICE OF DRACULA. ALL THESE LIVES I SHALL GIVE YOU — FROM NOW TILL TIME ETERNAL —

RENFIELD. Aaaaahhhhhhh!

VOICE OF DRACULA. ALL THESE LIVES AND MORE SHALL BE YOURS ... IF YOU WILL FALL DOWN AND WORSHIP ME! *(Renfield falls to his knees, crying.)*

RENFIELD. I am your servant!

VOICE OF DRACULA. NOW: BID ME ENTER! *(All sound stops, abruptly. Renfield takes a deep breath. He lifts the cup.)*

RENFIELD. Enter, my Lord and Master. *ENTER! (A crash of sound, as — Renfield tosses the steam from the cup into the air, and it instantly becomes a — burst of smoke. Lights flicker out, briefly. As the smoke clears ... and the lights restore ... Dracula is standing in the cell. Renfield instantly grovels at his feet.)* I have waited patiently, Master. I have waited with diligence for you. *(Dracula holds a large rat in one of his hands. He snaps the rat's neck and squeezes it with his hand, forcing blood to gush from it ... and fall onto Renfield's mouth and face.)*

DRACULA. And great shall be your reward. *(Instantly, another burst of smoke ... another flicker of light ... and Dracula is gone. Renfield cries out, looking around for him.)*

RENFIELD. Take me with you! Please please. Master! Take me! *(Lights shift to — the guest room. Night. The moon, of course, is full and prominent. Mina sits, holding a newspaper. She wears the rosary around her neck. Harker is putting on a coat, preparing to leave.)*

MINA. *(Looking at the newspaper.)* And here's another. That's three of them in two days.

HARKER. Missing like the others?

MINA. Yes. A little boy. Six years old. Found lost, disoriented, a bruise on his neck. Claiming, like the others, to have been snatched up by the "Bloofer Lady."

HARKER. How odd.

MINA. And on the day of Lucy's funeral — it's too much to bear. *(Approaching Harker, with great concern.)* Jonathan? *(He turns to her, his coat on.)* You've not told me where you're going.

HARKER. You're safe here, Mina.

MINA. That's not what I asked. We're to have no secrets. That is our pact. *(Pause.)* Now, it's nearly midnight, where are you going?

HARKER. I can't tell you.

MINA. Why?

HARKER. I've been asked not to.

MINA. By whom? *(Pause, desperately.)* Jonathan, please —

HARKER. By Professor Van Helsing. He's assured me that neither of us is in danger. But, Miss Lucy must be attended to, and the whereabouts of the Count must be discovered.

MINA. *Attended to* — what can that mean?! Lucy's been entombed for days. And not two hours ago we said our final prayers over her. *(Harker stares at her, then he takes her face in his hands.)* Jonathan, please — what is it?

HARKER. *(Quietly.)* You must trust in my silence, Mina. You must stay here where it is safe. *(He kisses her, gently, on the forehead — then leaves. She stares off after him. Music, as — Mina prepares for bed — turning back the covers of the bed; then, removing her dress, revealing a full white slip underneath. Then ... exactly like Lucy in Act One, Mina goes to the window and closes one side of the drapes. Then ... as music builds ... the other. Nothing jumps out. Mina steps toward the bed, as — The sound of a large door opening is heard, accompanied by music and the hissing and rattling of snakes — Mina looks around trying to locate the sound, as — a door in the center of the floor, opens; [or: light pours onstage*

58

from an previously unseen direction.] Music builds, as does the hiss-
ing and rattling. Mina turns, sees the door in the floor, and gasps
— she stands motionless, staring at the light pouring up, as — a
hand rises from the door and reaches out to her. She stares, frozen,
fearful ... then ... she slowly walks towards the light ... transfixed.
She stops, emblazoned by the light. She removes the rosary from her
neck and lets it slowly fall to the ground. She reaches out and takes
hold of the hand. Music and sound crescendo, as — Mina steps down
into the opening, and disappears below [or: offstage in the direction
of the light]. The door slams shut behind her, as music and sound
snap out and lights shift to — the cell. Renfield, staring front with
the dead eyes of an animal. He remains covered with the blood from
the rat. He is bound at the ankle and wrist as before.)
RENFIELD.   In all the great rounds of its daily course, the
sun rises on no life more miserable than mine. He has betrayed me! And mark these words — RIGHT NOW, turn to
the person next to you and borrow a pencil, for I shall not
say this again: One should rather die than be betrayed. There
is no deceit in death — it delivers precisely what it has promised. Betrayal, though ... betrayal is the *willful slaughter of hope.*
(He stands, suddenly:) IT SHALL NOT SIT. *(Lights snap out on*
Renfield, and shift to — Lucy's tomb. A raised stone sepulchre. It is
just before dawn. Van Helsing enters, carrying a lantern. He is fol-
lowed by Harker, who carries a large cloth bag in one hand, and a
Bible in the other. And, finally, by Seward.)
VAN HELSING.   Now, it is time. Now that the sun is about
to rise — let us look within. *(Van Helsing and Harker, using some*
tools from the bag, prepare to remove the stone slab which covers the
tomb. Seward stands at a distance. His coat or cape is draped over
his shoulders.)
SEWARD.   Never have I endured a more woeful night. Waiting in this graveyard for hours. And for what reason?!
VAN HELSING.   John, help us here. And may your eyes see
what your heart refuses. *(They push/lift the stone slab aside. They*
look down into the tomb.)
HARKER.   *(Softly.)* My god.
VAN HELSING.   It's as I feared. *(Seward reaches down in the*
tomb with his hands, frantically.)

SEWARD. What have you done with her? Answer me! In this very crypt I saw her laid, and — *(To Van Helsing.)* You're behind this, aren't you? And I, of all people — to not recognize madness when it stands before me!

VAN HELSING. John, listen to me —

SEWARD. With what malice do you lure the living to your purpose — and what ghastly plans do you inflict upon the dead?!

HARKER. Dr. Seward, calm yourself —

SEWARD. *(Overlapping.)* WHAT HAVE YOU DONE WITH HER?! *(Three simultaneous sounds: a child's scream, a loud rustle of branches, and the howl of a wolf. Van Helsing listens, then speaks, firmly.)*

VAN HELSING. You require more proof? Well, you shall have it. *(From the darkness, a Voice. [or: if amplified, the Voice can come from a changing variety of directions].)*

VOICE. *(An eerie sing-song.)* Little boy ... little boy ... come and see me ... little boy ...

HARKER.   VAN HELSING.
Who's there?   Hide now — back away and observe!

VOICE. I'm a friend of the children ... I'm the Bloofer Lady ... *(The men continue to look around, trying to find the Voice.)* Won't you come out and play? That would make the Bloofer Lady happy. *(Lucy appears behind them, at a distance. She wears a long, tattered white garment, streaked down the front with <u>fresh blood</u>. Around her neck hangs several strings of <u>children's shoes</u>. Her face is completely pale. Blood drips from the corners of her mouth. Her hair and eyes are wild, furious, desirous.)*

LUCY. Hi, there, Johnny. *(The men turn and see her.)* Want to be my little friend?

SEWARD. *(Stunned by her appearance.)* Lucy ... *(Harker unsheaths his knife, saying:)*

HARKER. Let me have at her —

VAN HELSING. *(Stopping Harker.)* There's no need. The sun is almost up.

LUCY. *(To Seward.)* Come to Lucy. My arms are so hungry for you. Be my husband, Johnny — come to me and let me be yours ... *(Seward takes a few steps toward her, transfixed.)*

VAN HELSING. That's not her, John — that's not the Lucy you know —

LUCY. Who knows you better, Johnny? Who's loved you all these years?

VAN HELSING. *(To Lucy.)* Deception, nothing more, and it shall not work —

LUCY. *I know your thoughts, Jack. (Lucy — still at a distance from Seward — reaches out her hand, as though touching one of his shoulders, and then the other ... and, as he reacts to her "touch" ... his coat/cape falls slowly from his shoulders.)* I know your wishes before you wish them. *(U., the huge sun can now be seen, <u>beginning to rise</u>. Lucy stands near the tomb. Seward steps closer to her.)*

SEWARD. What have they done to you?

LUCY. They've given me LIFE. Life eternal. Yours for a kiss, Johnny. It's all yours for a kiss.

VAN HELSING. *(A glance at the rising sun.)* Just another minute, John. The sun will be up and it will be safe —

LUCY. You still want me, Johnny, I know it ... *(Seward brings Lucy's <u>hand mirror</u> from his pocket. He holds it in front of him — trying to show Lucy her own face.)*

SEWARD. 'Tis not your beauty that is gone. 'Tis your soul. *(The mirror catches the first rays of sunlight and <u>reflects it directly into Lucy's eyes</u>. She screams, trying to shield her eyes.)*

LUCY. Noooo —

SEWARD. Your soul is what I loved! Where has it gone?! Answer me!

LUCY. No, Johnny, no more —

SEWARD. My love is become hate, and my desire — loathing!

LUCY. NOOOOOOOOO —

SEWARD. I COULD KILL YOU MYSELF — *(Van Helsing and Harker hold Seward back, as — the sunlight forces Lucy to retreat/ slump into the tomb, <u>out of sight</u>.)*

VAN HELSING.	HARKER.
ENOUGH, JACK, ENOUGH.	STEADY, NOW —

(Seward, exhausted, crying — collapses to the ground behind the tomb.)

VAN HELSING.   Keep faith, now. It's almost over. Soon you will see her as she was. *(To Harker.)* The tools, Mr. Harker. *(Music. Harker removes a large wooden stake from the bag. He hands it to Van Helsing. Then, he lifts a large hammer from the bag.)* If I could spare you any of it, my friend, I surely would.

SEWARD.   *(Not looking up.)* Let's be done with it. *(From a flat case which he carries in his breast pocket, Van Helsing produces the "host" — a white, holy communion wafer. He breaks it in two.)*

VAN HELSING.   The "host" — the holy bread shall sanctify her eternal bed. She will take her rest with the angels. *(He drops the pieces of the host down into the tomb, producing a quick burning/sizzling sound. He now readies the stake above her [unseen] heart. He looks at Harker, who holds the hammer.)* I shall place the point over her heart, and speak the holy words as you strike. *(As Harker steps forward, Seward says:)*

SEWARD.   No.

VAN HELSING.   John, we must — *(Seward stands, reaches out his hand, asking for the hammer.)*

SEWARD.   It was my hand that loved her best. And my hand that will deliver her. *(Seward takes the hammer from Harker. Van Helsing nods, then readies the stake. Harker lifts the Bible, and holds it, prominently. Music begins, as — Van Helsing speaks into the tomb.)*

VAN HELSING.   We come in peace, for the sake of our dear friend, Miss Lucy. May the Light of Heaven drive this wretched darkness from her soul. *(Seward lifts the hammer.)* In the name of the Father — *(A swelling crash of music — powerful and sacred — as — Seward <u>drives the stake</u>, and — <u>Lucy screams</u>, hideously, <u>her hand thrusting up out of the tomb toward the sky</u>.)* And of the Son — *(Another crash of music, as — Seward <u>drives the stake</u> a second time, as — <u>Lucy screams, her hand now back inside the tomb [unseen]</u>.)* And of the holy ghost. *(A final crash of music, as — Seward <u>drives the stake</u> a final time, and — <u>Lucy cries out</u> — then ... quiet. In the distance, a bell tolls mournfully, beautifully. The sun has now fully risen. A long silence, as the men catch their breath, gather their strength. There is <u>blood</u> on Van Helsing's hands.)* Look, now. Look on her face. *(They do. Seward wipes a tear from his eye.)*

HARKER. She is changed back.

VAN HELSING. No longer the Devil's concubine. She is the Lucy we loved, her sweetness and purity restored. *(To Seward.)* John. If you will ... kiss her, now, as she asked. And let this kiss send her to heaven. *(Seward looks at Van Helsing, then leans down into the tomb slowly ... and kisses [the unseen] Lucy. In the distance, the bell tolls a final time. When this is done, Van Helsing puts his arm around Seward, comforting him. Harker has moved away, still holding the bible.)* Mr. Harker and I will finish up here. Her mouth must be filled with garlic, then her head severed. One step of our work will then be done. What remains is the greater task: to locate the author of these, our sorrows, and rid him from the world.

HARKER. Professor.

VAN HELSING. Yes?

HARKER. As Miss Lucy screamed, the final time, I felt the Bible grow warm in my hands.

VAN HELSING. It is the power of the Lord.

HARKER. But this, further ... *(He holds the Bible out to Van Helsing.)* A word has been burned into the cover. *(Van Helsing and Seward look.)*

VAN HELSING. "Carfax." *(Van Helsing looks up at Harker.)*

HARKER. The Count's destination. An estate here in London.

VAN HELSING. You're certain?

HARKER. Yes, I am.

VAN HELSING. Miss Lucy's final gift to us! *(He turns to Seward who looks distraught.)* John, do you know of this estate? *(Seward says nothing.)* John, what is it?

SEWARD. *(With a look at Harker.)* Had we known, we might have saved Lucy.

VAN HELSING. I don't understand —

SEWARD. Carfax. *It adjoins the asylum.* He has been, all this time, in our midst!

HARKER. Mina — *(Crack of thunder/music, as — Harker rushes off, and a shaft of light discovers — the cell. Renfield — shackled, as before — standing, eyes closed, head looking to the heavens, in supplication. Suddenly, Renfield's eyes pop open. He breathes heavily. His head snaps down and looks at his lower abdomen, fervently. A strange, high-pitched sound is heard. Renfield begins to forcefully press his lower abdomen — ritually, rhythmically — with his hands, saying:)*

RENFIELD. Bird-blood ... feather-blood ... spider-blood ... fly-blood — *(He coughs, then still rhythmically, his hands move to below his ribs — continuing to press, forcefully.)* Bird-blood ... feather-blood ... spider-blood ... fly-blood — *(He coughs again — and now, his hands move to his throat, still pressing — his voice growing more hoarse, more choked.)* Bird — *(Cough.)* — feather — *(Cough.)* — *(He bends at the waist, doubling over, his hands still on his throat.)* Bird — *(Cough.)* — BIRD — *(And now, a huge cough — his face unseen to us — strange, high-pitched sound builds, and — Renfield stands up straight, holding something in the air, triumphantly. It is — a large wishbone [bigger than we think he could have possibly swallowed], glistening with saliva. He holds it up, focused on it feverishly.)* The mad are mad so long as they are chained. But, loosed and afoot, are they the rampant, wretched SANE. *(He grabs either side of the wishbone, eerily saying:)* Make a wish! *(He snaps the wishbone, which is accompanied by — the sound of a huge tree snapping in two and — another loud crack of thunder. Renfield mutters his familiar "yes yes good very good [etc.]" under the following actions: he quickly puts half the wishbone in his mouth, and — with the other half, he picks the locks of his chains. He rushes to the door of the cell. He tosses the first half of the wishbone away — takes the other half from his mouth and — uses it to unlock the door of the cell. He flings the door open, shouting:)* MASTER! *(He rushes from the cell, disappearing into the night, as lights shift to — the guest room. Day. The drapes are open. Mina sits, fully clothed, on the bed — reading a newspaper. Her face is more pale than before. Her hair ever-so slightly mussed. She wears a small, dark scarf around her neck. Harker rushes in, overlapping Renfield's exit line.)*

HARKER. Mina!

MINA. Jonathan, what is it?

HARKER. You're safe?

MINA. *(With a laugh.)* You assured me I would be. *(He is staring at her, breathing hard.)* Why? *(He kneels by the bed, taking her hand. Mina looks at him, curious.)* Jonathan —

HARKER.   I want us to be married.

MINA.   And we shall be. In two months. The plans are made.

HARKER.   *(With a sudden urgency.)* Now. I want us to be married now. I want us to partake of the holy bread and join our souls as man and wife.

MINA.   *(With a curious smile.)* But, my love, why now?

HARKER.   Should any harm befall us — either of us —

MINA.   Jonathan, I'm here. We're safe. *(He sees something on the floor in the room.)* What is it?

HARKER.   The rosary. *(She reaches for her neck, [truly] expecting it to be there. Harker lifts it from the floor and brings it to her.)*

MINA.   It must have fallen this morning, as I dressed. *(He puts it around her neck, once more.)* There. You see. All is well. *(Harker looks in her eyes as lights shift quickly to — a <u>silhouette on Mina</u>, as well as a shaft of light on — Van Helsing, speaking to the audience. He holds in his hand a wild, red rose. Next to him is his valise.)*

VAN HELSING.   As the days passed, I alone began to suspect the change in her. The skin growing more pale. The distant, listless gaze. In our efforts to protect Miss Mina, we had — too literally, I'm afraid — kept her in the dark. The deeper part of this secret is that she, herself, seemed unaware. A stranger to her own transformation. *(Lights expand now to reveal — the guest room. Night. The drapes are open — the moon looms, huge. Mina stands, looking over some papers. She is clearly <u>pale</u>. Van Helsing steps into the scene. Also present are Harker and Seward.)*

MINA.   Thank you for coming. I shall waste no time in making my point. And, if you feel I talk above my station, let the magnitude of circumstance be my apology. This darkness, this silence between us must come to an end. We must work together with absolute trust, and, in that way, be stronger as a group than we are alone. I have, these three nights, slept fitfully. I've heard noises in the dark, been plagued by disturbing dreams. You have been in search of the Count. So, too, I fear, *have I. (The men look at one another. She removes her scarf from her neck.)*

HARKER.   *(Softly.)* My god ...

MINA. I have no memory of it. But the marks are clear. Now, you must tell me: is this how Lucy died? Through some maladventure involving the Count? *Keep this from me no longer. (Harker and Seward look at Van Helsing.)* Professor? *(Music, under. Van Helsing looks at them all. He walks to the window and <u>closes</u> the drapes. Then, he stands before them in the room — still holding the wild rose in his hand.)*

VAN HELSING. There are such things as vampires. They are known everywhere that men have ever been. The *Nosferatu* have the strength of twenty men, and the ancient ones — like our Count Dracula — come armed with the cunning of the ages. He can transform himself into wolf or bat, mist or fog — any form of nature which suits him. He throws no shadow, can be seen in no mirror, and for sustenance, one thing only: the blood of the living. And when his special pabulum is plenty — he grows younger, his faculties stronger, his ghastly powers more vital by the hour —

MINA. *(Holding her neck.)* And to those bitten, his hunger brings death?

VAN HELSING. Death of goodness, yes. But, life eternal amid the damned. Those bitten — *repeatedly,* as I pray to our Lord you have not been — become the very thing which afflicted them: the disciples of the night. *(Mina grabs at Harker, who holds her tightly.)*

HARKER. But how could this change befall Mina? She is pure of heart, she is —

VAN HELSING. So, too, I'm afraid, was the Count. I have studied him for many years. In life, he was a man of the utmost virtue. *(Looking at Mina.)* The terror of it is, my friend, that this evil grows richest in a soul most pure. *(Music is gone. Harker speaks, forcefully, bitterly.)*

HARKER. You assured me she was safe here, Professor. You gave me your word.

VAN HELSING. His power, to this point, has bested our knowledge, but we shall —

HARKER. Waste no more of our time! I beg you, tell us directly: is there no way to defeat this monster?

VAN HELSING. Oh, there is a way, Mr. Harker. Dracula can

do all these many things ... but he is not free. He is shackled to the laws of the night: His power ceases — as does that of all evil things — at the coming of the day. *(He opens his valise.)* Certain objects hold a telling power over him: the garlic you know of, the bread of holy communion — *(He removes the flat case containing "the host" from his valise. Then, puts the case in his breast pocket.)* The holy cross of our Lord — *(Removes his large crucifix from the valise. He puts this, too, in the pocket of his coat.)* And, the branch of the wild rose, which, when placed on his coffin, serves to lock him fast within. *(Van Helsing hands the wild rose to Mina.)* He cannot — at first — enter any place unless someone who dwells there bid him enter —

SEWARD.   *(To Harker, an accusation.)* Meaning someone let him at Lucy —

HARKER.   *(Similarly.)* And at Mina —

VAN HELSING.   And, most to the moment, he must each day sleep in his native soil or he will die.

HARKER.   The digging —

VAN HELSING.   Exactly. That is what you heard at his castle. Boxes of *Transylvanian soil* being filled — boxes that are here now, in London.

SEWARD.   The ship's log notes the Count's cargo as fifty boxes — and just today, at Carfax, the Professor and I discovered forty-eight of them.

VAN HELSING.   I sanctified the soil of each — making them of no use to the Count. When we find the remaining two boxes, we shall find the man himself! Finally, these words above all others: If we in this room fail, our fate is not one of mere life or death. It is that *we become as him,* foul things of the night — without heart, without conscience, preying on the quivering bodies of those we love best. If we fail: to us, forever, are the gates of heaven shut. Look now to your own hearts, and answer: Are we to cower in the face of such adversity? Or are we, as Miss Mina has so bravely said, to rise up and hunt this wretch to his true death?! *(Van Helsing's eyes scan the faces of the others. Then, he goes to the center of the room and kneels on one knee, bows his head — and extends the crucifix in front of him. One by one, Harker ... then Seward ... then, fi-*

nally ... Mina gradually join Van Helsing — kneeling near him, putting their hands on the crucifix, forming a circle of prayer. Behind them, unseen to them ... <u>a hand very slowly emerges through the drapes. The hand parts the drapes ever-so-slightly.</u> This happens as Van Helsing speaks.) With a steadfast belief in science, a fierce reliance on faith, and the avid hope that there remains in us light enough to dispel the darkness ... we pledge our whole selves.

HARKER, SEWARD, and MINA. *(Softly, heads bowed.)* Amen. *(The hand vanishes, the drapes fall closed once again, as — Van Helsing stands.)*

VAN HELSING. We have sealed now either the end of ourselves — or the death knell of the Count. Now, to our plan. The remaining boxes must be found, and upon — *(As Mina is attempting to stand, she collapses to the ground, weakly. Harker quickly takes her in his arms.)*

MINA. Jonathan ...

HARKER. She's no strength at all. *(Sound of <u>glass breaking</u> behind the drapes. Seward rushes to the window and <u>throws open</u> the drapes — there is nothing there.)*

SEWARD. Nothing.

VAN HELSING. Quickly, now. She has lost more blood than we imagined. Move her to the bed. *(Music. Mina has now completely passed out. Harker and Seward move her to the bed. Van Helsing rushes to his bag, giving orders to Seward.)* John, make him ready. I shall need at his veins. *(Seward begins to rip Harker's sleeve from his shirt, as — Van Helsing rushes to Harker with the <u>blood transfusion device</u>. Van Helsing and Seward quickly swab the arms of Mina and Harker, insert the needles and hook up the tubes between them. — Harker stares at all this in disbelief.)*

HARKER. Professor Van Helsing —

VAN HELSING. Breathe now and hold steady. You are giving her the life which he has stolen! *(Music builds, as — an Attendant rushes in, holding a shattered pair of ankle chains. He yells to Seward.)*

ATTENDANT. He's gone, sir! He's escaped!

SEWARD. Who?

ATTENDANT. Renfield. He's left the asylum —

SEWARD. *(Urgently.)* Did he mention his Master — did he use that word?

ATTENDANT. Well, yes, he did —

SEWARD. He will lead us to the Count! Professor, come!

VAN HELSING. *(Overseeing the transfusion.)* I can't leave here —

SEWARD. You alone know his mind — you alone can confront him!

VAN HELSING. John —

SEWARD. Hurry, now — there's no time to waste — *(Van Helsing turns quickly back to Harker.)*

VAN HELSING. Mr. Harker, you must —

HARKER. Go, Professor — before it's too late — *(Seward grabs the crucifix, as Van Helsing continues to stare at Harker and Mina.)*

SEWARD. Now, Professor — *(Seward rushes out.)*

HARKER. YOU MUST GO — *(Van Helsing turns and rushes out, following Seward. Music builds. Harker looks down at Mina, as, from a heretofore unknown direction [down from the ceiling? through a panel?] — Renfield appears. His appearance is at its maddest. He holds a beautiful violin. Harker stares at him, terrified, confused.)*

RENFIELD. All day and all night do I wait! But — NOTHING. Promises of bloody creatures teeming with life. But — NOTHING. NOT EVEN A MEASLY LITTLE *BLOW-FLY* — NOTHING!

HARKER. *(Overlapping.)* Professor — Dr. Seward — someone come quickly — *(Harker is stranded, still tethered by the blood-tube to Mina, unable to do anything about Renfield — who has not even noticed the others. Renfield plays a quick manic little phrase on his violin with an imaginary bow — as he sings the notes of the phrase.)*

RENFIELD. I WAS TO BE YOURS, MASTER! I WAS TO SERVE YOU THROUGH THE AGES! *(He throws himself to the floor, as he plays/sings another quick manic phrase on the violin.)*

HARKER. *(Calling off.)* Is anyone there — please help us!

RENFIELD. I TRIED TO WARN THEM — I TRIED BUT THEY DON'T LISTEN. *(A quick shift, bitterly.)* He's nothing but a wanton sailor with a cape. *(Looks to Mina.)* He will keep his promises to HER — she will get HER life — she will get HER blood — because she is BEAUTIFUL — because she PLEASES HIM — because he can SKEWER HER WITH HIS TEETH.

HARKER. *(Overlapping.)* Professor — someone — in here — please — come quickly — *(As Renfield speaks, the floor beneath him begins to rise [or: as before, light pours onstage from off.] This is the door which opened earlier — but this time we see the <u>entire piece</u> which is, of course — a large wooden box. <u>It rises fully into the room</u>. It is identical to the one we saw in Act One. Renfield speaks, unaware, as the box <u>lifts him</u>. Mina is beginning to awaken.)*

RENFIELD. BUT WHAT OF THE REST OF US? WHAT OF THE *GREAT UN-BEAUTIFUL MULTITUDES*? WHAT OF US BORN HIDEOUS — BLESSED ONLY WITH HONEST DEVOTION? IT IS *WE* WHO LOVE YOU! MORE TRULY, MORE DEEPLY THAN SHE! *(He <u>begins to play/sing another phrase on the violin</u>, as — the door of the box opens — throwing Renfield aside. Renfield stares into the light pouring from the box. Mina stands on the bed, also facing the light. Harker, growing weaker from the constant loss of blood, struggles to stand also. He looks on, shocked, horrified. Renfield, still holding his violin, throws himself to his knees.)* Master, forgive me! I will do your bidding! *(Music continues — stranger and stranger, as — Dracula emerges from the box [or: enters from the direction of the light]. Renfield throws himself at Dracula's feet, grovels furiously.)* I will follow you, Master! To the ends of earth and beyond! Please, forget not me, your servant! Forget not I — who love you! Forget not — *(As Renfield speaks, Dracula holds out his hand, asking for the violin. Renfield, kneeling, happily hands it to him. Dracula stands behind Renfield.)* I never doubted you, Master! I knew you'd return — I knew you'd not forsake me — I knew there was a place for me in your kingdom — a holy — *(A screech of furious music, as — In an instant Dracula pulls the strings away from one end of the violin and <u>wraps them around Renfield's neck</u> — strangling him. Renfield screams and gasps ... and then, just before Renfield is about to collapse ... Dracula <u>releases him</u>. Dracula hands the violin to the still-kneeling, barely conscious Renfield. Renfield looks up at Dracula — a gentle smile on his face, thankful to be spared death — as Dracula takes Renfield's head in his hands. Music fades down. A pause, then — Dracula <u>snaps Renfield's neck in one quick move</u>, kill-*

ing him instantly. [The popping of a small piece of unseen 'bubble-wrap' in Renfield's hand can produce the desired sickening sound.] Still on the bed, Mina screams. Harker is kneeling beside the bed now, weaker still. Dracula — at a distance from them — turns very slowly to Mina.)

DRACULA.   Miss Mina, my beautiful flower ...

MINA.   *(Breathless, terrified.)* What are you?

DRACULA.   *(Approaching her.)* I have dined with kings. I have commanded nations. I have watched Time chisel lines into the faces of young women. But, Time shall never scar you with its hand. You are for the ages.

HARKER.   *(Managing a sound.)* The *rosary* — Mina — *(Mina begins to lift the rosary in Dracula's direction, but — Dracula rips it from her neck and holds it, a fierce look in his eyes.)*

DRACULA.   Toys! Why must you try my patience with your petty toys?! *(He hurls the rosary across the room.)* I'm no longer the weak man you met in Transylvania, Mr. Harker. Your gift of England has made me strong. *I quite like it here.* One could, it seems, return again and again and never get one's fill.

HARKER.   *(Struggling to his feet, still tethered to Mina.)* Stay away from her —

DRACULA.   Mr. Harker, please — you know how I prize civility. Another sound and I shall have to feed her your brains. *(Harker gathers enough strength to pull his knife from its sheath.)*

HARKER.   Let her be — let her be or I shall — *(Dracula extends his fingers toward Harker — hypnotizing him.)*

DRACULA.   And, thank you for the use of your knife. *(He twists his fingers — causing the knife to turn in Harker's hand ... and offer itself up to Dracula.)* It suits my purpose. *(He lifts the knife and cuts the blood tube — near Harker's arm. He pinches the open end. Then, he snaps his fingers, once — and Harker collapses to the floor. Out cold. Dracula, holding the blood tube, looks at Mina — who stares at him, horrified — not seduced.)* Ah, sweet Mina. *(Mina tries to yank the blood tube from her arm.)*

MINA.   No — you won't — *(But before she can do this, Dracula begins to suck on the other end of the tube. Mina cries out in anguish, then falls back on the bed, writhing, her strength being drained from her. After a moment, Dracula drops the tube. He gently pulls*

71

the end of the tube from Mina's arm. He touches the mark with his finger ... and gently licks the spilt blood from her arm. He is behind her on the bed now, holding her in his arms.)

DRACULA. Yes, I quite like it here. The men of England live lives of order and reason. Not a ripple disturbs the still surface of their complacency. *(A wry smile.)* But standing water grows fetid, you see — giving rise to disease. The complacent man is my puppet. And his lover, my bride.

MINA. But why me? Only tell me — what have I done?

DRACULA. *(Looking down at her.)* You are their treasure. You stir their dreams, leaving envy in your wake. All of them, Mina, not just your betrothed — *all* of them desire your love. And now you — their best, beloved flower — are mine: blood of my blood, flesh of my flesh, kin to my kin ... my beautiful, bountiful wine-press. *(He lifts his head, revealing his <u>fanged teeth</u>. He slowly, deliciously, <u>bites her neck</u>. She cries out achingly, and gasps, grabbing at the bed. A beautiful, mournful wolf howl joins the music. Dracula pulls away from her, breathing heavily, sated with pleasure. Mina lies limply on the bed, eyes still open.)* You are weak now, but here is strength. *(He opens his shirt and reveals his chest.)* Here is sustenance. *(He touches his chest with one finger.)* Here is life. *(He <u>slashes</u> his long fingernail across his chest, <u>drawing blood</u>, as — all sound stops, instantly. In <u>complete silence</u>, he takes Mina's hand. She rises, kneeling on the bed, facing him. She looks at his bleeding chest. She looks up into his eyes. He speaks, very softly.)* Drink. And be mine. *(She slowly moves her head toward his chest. She puts her mouth near the blood. <u>She licks the blood, very slowly, with her tongue ... once</u>. She looks up at him. He nods. She returns her mouth to his chest ... and now <u>buries her face in the wound, drinking the blood from his body</u>. He throws his head back with pleasure.)* When I but whisper "come to me" — you shall travel the ages to do my bidding. You will cross oceans of time. *(Suddenly, music returns, as — Seward and Van Helsing rush in. Dracula pulls Mina away from his chest.)*

SEWARD. My god —

VAN HELSING. Our theory is proved fact —

SEWARD. *(With venom, to the Count.)* What have you done to them?

DRACULA. Why, I've done all that I can. *(Gesturing to Harker, Mina, and Renfield.)* Given rest to one, food to another, and heaven to a third. *(Seward rushes at Dracula, trying to pull Mina from him.)*

SEWARD. LET HER GO — *(With one hand, Dracula grabs Seward and throws him across the room. He lands on the ground, dazed. Van Helsing, holding the "host" in his hand, approaches Dracula slowly.)*

VAN HELSING. The soil of your homeland has been sanctified by God — box after box after box —

DRACULA. *(A hideous growl.)* Noooooo —

VAN HELSING. Your coffin-home has been destroyed — *(Dracula moves away, as Mina collapses back onto the bed — her mouth and face wet with fresh blood. Dracula stands near the window. Van Helsing removes his crucifix from his coat and holds it behind his back — unseen to Dracula.)*

DRACULA. You shall yet be sorry — each and every one of you! My revenge has just begun!

VAN HELSING. You've nowhere left to hide —

DRACULA. Eternity shall comfort me —

VAN HELSING. Your time is drawing near —

DRACULA. The centuries shall be my home! *(Music builds, as — Van Helsing continues to approach Dracula.)*

VAN HELSING. "Truly my soul waiteth upon God: from him cometh my salvation."

DRACULA. Do not mock me with your FOOLISH PRAYERS —

VAN HELSING. "They consult to cast him down, they delight in lies —"

DRACULA. FAITH HAS MADE YOUR LOVERS MY JACKALS —

VAN HELSING. "But in God is my salvation and glory, he is my defense, I shall not be moved —"

DRACULA. *(Overlapping.)* IT HAS SOFTENED YOUR THROAT FOR THE HUNGER OF MY WILL! *(Van Helsing thrusts the crucifix in front of Dracula.)*

VAN HELSING. "FOR THE LORD GOD HAS SPOKEN —!" *(Instantly, the stage goes dark and — [if possible] the crucifix bursts into flames. Van Helsing stares at it, shocked, as — Dracula's am-*

plified voice is heard.)

VOICE OF DRACULA. *(With a cold deliciousness.)* He has spoken. But he has not been heard. *(The lights have now restored in the room, and — Dracula is gone. Van Helsing rushes for the window, throws open the drapes, and* <u>there is nothing there</u>. *The window remains barred, seemingly untouched.)*

SEWARD. No sight of him?!

VAN HELSING. A hundred white wolves, running to the sea — and becoming, with each step, mist. Fog. Disappearing on the horizon. *(Harker begins to awake, seeing — Mina, eyes wide open, leaning limply against the bed, fresh blood on her lips and face. Music and sound have faded down, out.)*

HARKER. *(Bewildered.)* My god, what is here? What has happened? *(Seward goes to him.)*

SEWARD. It's safe now, he's gone — *(Harker is gaining clarity now, and with it, horror. He rushes to Mina.)*

HARKER. Mina! Oh, God help her, what has happened? This blood — is this his handiwork? *(Pause, the men stare at him, he turns to Seward.)* Answer me!

MINA. Jonathan ... *(Harker goes to her.)* Stay with me.

HARKER. I'm here, Mina ... *(She holds onto him tightly, burying her face on his chest. He holds her in his arms.)*

SEWARD. *(Looking at the corpse of Renfield.)* For years I wanted nothing more than access to the soul of a madman. Had I but known ...

VAN HELSING. Amid this misery have we learned something: Notwithstanding his powers, he *fears us.*

SEWARD. How can you say that?!

VAN HELSING. He fears time! He fears want! If not — why his hurried escape? The heart of our plan — the destruction of his ancient soil — is sound! *(Van Helsing breaks a piece of the "host" and drops it into the wooden box in the room.)* This box here counts as forty-nine —

HARKER. But there is still one left.

VAN HELSING. And that, I propose, is for *traveling.*

SEWARD. To where?

VAN HELSING. To where else? His home, the soil he must have to survive! *(Mina pulls her head away from Harker's chest —*

and sees the <u>blood</u> from her mouth on his shirt. She touches the blood on her mouth and chin.)

MINA.   Oh, Jonathan. I am unclean. *(Pulling away, standing.)* You must never touch me, or kiss me again. Such cruel fate, that I am to be feared by you — whom I love most of all!

HARKER.   Mina, I will —

MINA.   There is poison in me — an insurrection in my soul that will lead god knows where. But this above all must you promise me: that if his influence wins me, if I am so changed that I enter the blackest parts of the world and become a beast such as he — *you must kill me.*

HARKER.   SEWARD.

Never —   No —

MINA.   Without remorse — without hesitation —

HARKER.   Do not ask this of me!

MINA.   You must kill me! I am infected by this enemy — his blood on my lips, his blood in my veins — *(She stops, suddenly, looking at the veins in her arm.)*

HARKER.   Mina? *(Mina looks up at Seward.)*

MINA.   And my blood in his. *(Turns quickly to Seward.)* Dr. Seward.

SEWARD.   What is it?

MINA.   Hypnotize me.

SEWARD.   What?

MINA.   You know the procedure, don't you. Lucy told me —

SEWARD.   Well, yes, but I —

MINA.   There *is* a way to know his plans and thus track him, safely.

VAN HELSING.   What way is that?

MINA.   Through his own blood. *Through me.* (Mina looks to Van Helsing.)

VAN HELSING.   Yes! We have been blind — but Miss Mina has helped us to see. We, too, have powers — and let them now be marshaled against him. Jack, do as she asks — through her let us know his thoughts. *(Seward steps D. and stands behind Mina, passing a pencil back and forth past her eyes, slowly. Van Helsing turns to Harker.)* Mr. Harker, prepare passage for us — for it is you who've been to where I suspect we're headed. To

Transylvania! To the lair of the Count! *(Huge crack of thunder. Music and wind/rain under, as the stage narrows to — three shafts of light, D.: Mina and Seward in one; Van Helsing in the second; Harker in the third. As they speak, the attendants/maids enter behind them and give them their traveling coats/capes, etc., as well as the large cloth bag containing their tools.)*

SEWARD. *(To Mina, continuing the hypnosis.)* Look now — deep within your mind — what is there?

MINA. Darkness, nothing more —

HARKER. *(To the audience.)* And now, the four of us heading east — aboard the Orient Express —

VAN HELSING. *(Also to the audience.)* I had the men write their wills before we left. This is no idle precaution —

SEWARD. *(To Mina, but no longer passing the pencil before her eyes.)* And now, what is there? The same?

MINA. Yes. Darkness close at hand. A musty smell around me —

SEWARD. The Count in his coffin! It is working —

MINA. And beyond, the sound of waves, still pounding and pounding —

HARKER. The hypnosis reveals the Count traveling by boat.

VAN HELSING. So, we proceed overland — by train — to reach Varna before he does —

SEWARD. Days later, and still the same —

MINA. No, there is a change: the waves have stopped. And, now, footsteps. Voices —

SEWARD. He's reached the port.

HARKER. And we are here, at Varna, waiting for him —

SEWARD. Where is he?!

HARKER. Searching the ship, high and low —

SEWARD. Nothing —

HARKER. But he has tricked us —

SEWARD. He's sailed to another port — ! *(They turn and speak to one another from their shafts of light.)*

VAN HELSING. That is the risk of the hypnosis, friends. It may *work both ways.* He may know *our* thoughts through Miss Mina —

MINA. Water again. But, not crashing. A softer sound —

76

SEWARD.   He's traveling by river —

MINA.   Yes, a river! That's it, that's the sound —

HARKER.   The Sereth — I know of it from my travels. It runs round the Borgo pass — *(Harker and Mina are now at Van Helsing's side.)*

VAN HELSING.   And to the Castle!

SEWARD.   I'll procure a ship and follow him on the water —

VAN HELSING.   Yes, and take Mr. Harker with you —

HARKER.   And what of Mina?

VAN HELSING.   I will take her to the Castle!

HARKER.   Have you gone mad?!

VAN HELSING.   SHE ALONE can lead us! SHE ALONE will take us to the heart of his crypt — and once there, we shall effect his demise!

HARKER.   Not for the world will I let you do this! Not by Heaven or by Hell!

MINA.   Say no more!

VAN HELSING.   She is our greatest weapon in this —

HARKER.   Do you know what that place is?

MINA.   I beg of you both — *say no more!*

HARKER.   *(Overlapping.)* Have you been inside that hellish den, where grisly shapes appear in every speck of dust? Answer me, Professor —

VAN HELSING.   Mr. Harker, I —

HARKER.   YOU HAVE NOT FELT HIS HUNGRY LIPS UPON YOUR THROAT!

VAN HELSING.   I TAKE HER THERE TO SAVE HER!

MINA.   PLEASE — *(They stop and turn to her.)* He is listening even now. And through me, he knows your every word. So, please, if you hold me in your hearts, *say no more.* From this moment on, *tell me nothing. (Mina moves away into a light, separate from the others. Van Helsing and Harker stare at each other.)*

VAN HELSING.   Well, Mr. Harker?

HARKER.   On your own soul does this lie. *(The huge sun is fully visible U. now. From this moment on, it remains prominent — slowly setting. It is not completely gone until noted. The actors address the audience once again, as the — music builds.)*

SEWARD.   We are on the river now. Mr. Harker and I, following the Count's ship —

MINA.   And the Professor and I by wagon, to the Castle —

VAN HELSING.   *(Looking at Mina.)* Miss Mina's internal struggle is unmistakable.

MINA.   At sunrise, this weakness in me — but then, at sunset, this *strength*, this *hunger* —

VAN HELSING.   I can see the vampire taking hold within her —

MINA.   My mouth so dry. My gums sore from the force of my teeth, coming alive in my mouth —

HARKER.   May God make us ministers of this monster's destruction —

MINA.   *(With great fear.)* What changes are here, that my body welcomes what my mind most fears? *(Mina's light snaps out — she is gone. The men do not see her leave.)*

SEWARD.   And now: the Count's boat heading for shore — docking —

VAN HELSING.   The Castle now in sight —

HARKER.   THERE IS THE BOX!

SEWARD.   The wooden box being placed on a wagon, hitched to a team —

VAN HELSING.   The Castle door reached. And, in the distance, a wagon approaching — a wagon with *no driver* at its head —

HARKER.   Horses procured and we give chase, the last light of day fading —

VAN HELSING.   We must take him in his coffin before the light is gone —

SEWARD.   We ride at a fury, WE ARE RACING THE SUNSET —

HARKER.   At the Castle door his carriage stops —

VAN HELSING.   His wagon pulls away, and there —

SEWARD.   There before us is the object of our chase — *(The storm abates, the music fades, as lights reveal — the wooden box. It sits on a pile of ancient stones near the entrance to the Castle. The huge sun is <u>nearly gone from view</u>.)*

VAN HELSING.   Quickly, the sun is nearly gone —

HARKER.   Mina — *(The men look around: Mina is gone.)* What have you done with her?!

VAN HELSING.   Let us settle first with the Count, before its too late —

HARKER.   Professor —!

SEWARD.   Harker, help me — *(Seward and Harker take tools from a bag and remove the lid from the box. They look within. Light [perhaps] pours up from inside the box.)*

HARKER.   The man himself.

SEWARD.   Hurry now — *(They set the lid aside. Van Helsing has taken the case from his pocket and is dropping numerous communion wafers — the "host" — in a large circle around the box. This sacred circle is further accented by lighting.)*

VAN HELSING.   This sacred circle will keep him at bay should he escape the coffin. He can not pass over the holy bread.

HARKER.   The SUN IS GONE — *(And, it is gone — an ominous dark moonlight filling the stage.)*

VAN HELSING.   Quickly! *(Van Helsing readies a large stake and hammer. All three men are now near the box — inside the "sacred circle.")*

SEWARD.   THE STAKE — HERE — *(As Van Helsing hands Seward the stake. Harker grabs the hammer.)*

VAN HELSING.   NOW, MR. HARKER — *(As Harker lifts the hammer to strike — strange music plays, accompanied by hissing, rattling and whispered breathing, as — the vixens appear. And now ... there are three of them — Mina is one of them — her hair wild, her face white, red lips and fanged teeth. The Vixens approach the men — trapping them inside the sacred circle with the box.)*

MINA.   *(To Harker.)* Come to me, my love. Won't you come and be my husband? My bridesmaids have brought me to the altar. *(The Vixens hiss and coo.)* Now, Jonathan — I'm ready to marry you now. *(The other two Vixens reach and grab at Seward and Van Helsing from outside the sacred circle — but they can't get inside the circle. They wince in anger and pain whenever they try to step/reach over the "host." Mina approaches Harker — who stands near the box.)*

HARKER.   Mina, it's not too late, we can save you, we can —

MINA.   Now, Jonathan. There are no secrets between us now.

(Mina picks up a holy wafer from the sacred circle. She cries out as it burns her hand — but she does not let go.) Here is the holy bread! If you truly love me, marry me now —

VAN HELSING.   *(To Harker.)* Away — back away —!

HARKER.   *(Stepping toward Mina.)* Mina — *(Huge burst of sound, as — Dracula rises, instantly, from the box. The Vixens reach inside the circle and grab Van Helsing and Seward — pulling them outside the circle and restraining them. Harker, too, falls outside the circle — his knife falling to the ground Mina remains standing, facing Dracula — her back to us.)*

DRACULA.   Come to me. Marry yourself to me. *(Mina begins to walk slowly toward Dracula. She extends her open, empty hands in front of her — "giving herself" to him. The men shout their lines from the periphery of the circle, still restrained by the Vixens, still helpless.)*

HARKER.   MINA, DON'T —

DRACULA.   You are my bride. *(Mina keeps approaching him.)*

SEWARD.   MINA, BE STRONG —

DRACULA.   We shall travel the ages together. *(Mina nods, as she reaches him. He remains standing in the box.)*

VAN HELSING.   "IN GOD IS MY SALVATION AND MY GLORY — *(Mina is face to face with Dracula now — her back still to us. He takes her face in his hands and prepares to kiss her.)*

HARKER.   MINA, NO —

VAN HELSING.   *(Overlapping.)* "MY STRENGTH AND MY REFUGE IS IN GOD!" *(Music crescendos, as — Dracula and Mina kiss, then, instantly:)*

DRACULA.   *(In a thunderous, painful rage.)* AAAAAAAAAAA-AAAAHHHHHHHHHHHHHHHHHHHHHH!!!!!!! *(Mina turns from Dracula … and pulls the holy wafer from her mouth. She holds it into the air, saying:)*

MINA.   The holy bread!

VAN HELSING.   Praise be to God! *(At the same moment — Van Helsing frees himself from the Vixen holding him. Seward and Harker rush in, as well.)*

HARKER.   *Now — (Before Dracula can recover: Seward has pushed him back down in the box — Van Helsing has readied the stake — Harker has raised the hammer, about to drive the stake.)*

VOICE OF DRACULA.   *(From the box.)* NNNNNNNOOOOO-

OOOOOOO!!!!!!! *(Music reaches its zenith, as — Harker drives the stake — once — with all his might, and — <u>a stream of blood shoots into the air for a brief moment</u>, [or: a burst of red vapor rises into the air] and then — calm. The light inside the box vanishes. The music has faded away. The Vixens have disappeared. Harker, Van Helsing and Seward stand— exhausted, relieved, <u>stained with blood</u>. Mina stands, apart from the other, looking at the box. Long silence.)*

VAN HELSING.   *(Quietly.)* It's over. Our work has not been in vain. *(Harker is looking across the distance at Mina. Seward and Van Helsing lift the lid to the box and place it on the box. As they are about to slide it fully into place — to cover the "head" of the box — Mina says:)*

MINA.   *(Softly.)* We should, I think, have some sympathy for the hunted. *(The men stop. They turn and look at her.)*

HARKER.   Mina ...

MINA.   His misery is the saddest of all. His soul, too, must be saved. *(Mina steps away from the box and lifts something from the ground. It is a wild red rose.)*

HARKER.   We have sent him to eternal Hell where he belongs —!

VAN HELSING.   *(Overlapping, trying to quiet him.)* Mr. Harker, please, let her speak —

MINA.   For someday, I, too, may need such compassion. *(Pause.)* Would you then, had *I* been so guilty, deny salvation to me? *(Silence. Mina takes a deep breath — inhaling the fragrance of the rose.)*

VAN HELSING.   *(Quietly.)* She's right. *(Van Helsing picks up Harker's knife from the ground.)* Our work is but half complete. *(Van Helsing steps toward the box with the knife, as — Mina reaches out her empty hand — asking for the knife. Van Helsing stares at her ... then, he gives Mina the knife. She hands him the rose.)*

MINA.   *(Slowly, simply.)* He must be to Heaven sent. *(Music, as — Mina approaches the [uncovered] "head" of the box, holding the knife. The men look on. Mina looks up to the heavens, then clasps the knife strongly with two hands. Music builds, as — Mina lifts the knife over her head. The amplified voice of Dracula is heard, faintly, distantly.)*

VOICE OF DRACULA. *(A whisper.)* Mina … *(She plunges the knife down into the box and then — in one long, strong move — she pulls it from one side of the box to the other … severing Dracula's [unseen] head. There is a rush of wind as she does this, as though she has unleashed a great force. This sound gradually changes to — a strong, constant wind, which continues under. Music fades away. Mina steps back from the box, exhausted, her hands bloody. Resolutely, and with the last of her strength, she says:)* Now … and only now … is our work complete. *(Van Helsing looks at her. Nods. Then, he places the rose atop the box's lid. Silence. Harker looks at Mina. They move toward each other. She puts her head on his chest, her arms around him. He looks down at her neck.)*

HARKER. The marks on your neck, Mina. They're gone. Completely gone.

VAN HELSING. God be praised. *(Pause.)* And may you now — Mina and Jonathan — be rightfully joined in His name. *(Mina and Harker hold each other tightly. A church bell begins to toll, mournfully, beautifully.)* May these unholy hours serve only to strengthen your resolve; and may the light of love vanquish all fear. For now, and forever. *(Mina and Harker kiss, tenderly, tearfully. Then, arm in arm … they walk away and are gone. Seward is slowly gathering up the tools, etc. He looks down into the "head" of the box which remains uncovered.)*

SEWARD. Gone. The skin, the hair, the bones, the very man himself — *(He reaches into the box and lifts out a handful of grey ash. He lets it fall through his fingers back into the box.)* — all crumbled into dust and gone. *(Van Helsing and Seward slowly slide the lid completely into place — sealing the box. The rose remains on top. Van Helsing crosses himself, saying:)*

VAN HELSING. The God of light has emerged victorious. *(Seward and Van Helsing shake hands firmly, with finality … then Seward lifts the cloth bag and exits, slowly, as — Van Helsing turns to the audience.)* But, there is no joy in such a victory. For the web of darkness is constantly being woven. From the ashes of conquest is born revenge. *(A distant boys choir is heard, as — the bell continues to toll softly, beautifully.)* And so we vow to remain vigilant. What we have seen with our own eyes, and heard with our own ears, shall stay with us always. Not as memory

82

— but as *living truth.* *(Van Helsing takes one final look at the box, then turns and goes, as — the bell tolls a final time, and — lights fade to black.)*

END OF PLAY

Curtain Call

Music and lights up, as — the cast — everyone except Dracula — enters. Renfield holds the covered silver platter we've seen earlier. Individual bows, etc., Then — Renfield removes the cover, and there, of course is — Dracula's severed head/skull — garnished, of course, with wild roses. With Renfield's help, the head takes a bow. A full company bow, then music under, as Renfield quiets the audience and speaks to them.

RENFIELD.   We are, all of us, grateful for your patronage. And we bid you this one, final thought: There are dark imaginings in the world. *(He looks down at the head/skull.)* And, though a *foe* — when vanquished — is gone from sight ... *(He looks up at the audience, deliciously.)* A *fear* — once rooted in your mind — is *yours forever.* *(Renfield smiles devilishly, and gestures off, saying:)* Sweet dreams! *(Music back up, as — Dracula appears, in the flesh, with a flourish. Dracula takes his bow, then joins the rest of the cast for — one final company bow. Lights out, as — music plays the audience home.)*

[The following appeared in the playbill for the premiere of DRACULA at the Arizona Theatre Company in the spring of 1995.]

PLAYWRIGHT'S NOTE

I write to you from the midst of an enormous shadow. It is a shadow cast by history and fate; legend and myth. It is the shadow of Bram Stoker.

Stoker was a man of the theatre, serving as noted actor Henry Irving's business and tour manager for more than twenty-five years. It is altogether fitting, then, that DRACULA has found a home not only in book stores, but on the stage. Even more so than film (cursed by its technology to always present a full picture) the stage presents an audience with the exact conundrum faced by a reader of Stoker's book: pieces of a story; fragments and clues, left partly unassembled. Events awaiting a detective.

Most of the characters in Bram Stoker's DRACULA spend the better part of the book trying desperately — with the absolute best of intentions — to keep secrets from one another. Their reasons have to do with safety, honor, respectability, and science ... but every secret buys the vampire in their midst more time. Every evasion increases the impossibility of anyone assembling the totality of the facts, the cumulative force of the information. Secrecy breeds invasion. Darkness begets darkness.

It is this secrecy among the principal characters — heightened by the lack of third-person objectivity, since the novel consists entirely of personal letters, diaries, and news reports — that is the heart of the book's unique power. The objectivity so desperately needed by the characters is handed to the *reader*. A transcontinental jigsaw puzzle. A myriad of disturbing clues. And it falls to the reader alone to make the connections between these events.

The theatre's intrinsic reliance on the imagination of its audience (where one flower can represent a garden; one flag, a country) finds its perfect compliment in Stoker's DRACULA. Stoker, like the greatest of playwrights, understands that the mind is constantly in search of order. We cannot help but make stories out of whatever [seemingly] random information is presented to us. We are unwitting conspirators to the art of story telling. In this way, Stoker gives us the feeling that *the story cannot happen without us.*

I had a blast adapting Mr. Stoker's masterpiece. It was a thrilling, humbling, invigorating experience. As I was writing, my friends kept asking what my "take" on the story was. In my adaptation, they wondered, what did Dracula "represent?" And though I was tempted to join them in their esoteric aerobics, I realized that, for my purposes, to make Dracula a "metaphor" was cheating. It was akin to putting a muzzle on the most terrifying aspect of the story. You can hide from a metaphor. A metaphor doesn't wait outside your window under a full moon. A metaphor doesn't turn into a bat and land on your bed. So, instead, I took Mr. Stoker at his word: Although there are obviously many metaphorical dimensions to Count Dracula, the *actual being* is the most haunting. The question, then, is not what Dracula represents, but what he *is:* A brilliant, seductive, fanged beast waiting to suck the blood from your throat. Hide from that.

So, as the Count himself would say: "Welcome to my house! Enter freely and of your own will!" The shadow has been cast. The clues are here. The story awaits you.

What will happen tonight?

Steven Dietz
15 March 95
Seattle

PROPERTY LIST

ACT ONE

Dinner setting for one (RENFIELD, DRACULA) with:
      napkin
      wine glass
Wine glass (WAITER)
Photograph (RENFIELD)
Covered silver platter (WAITER) with:
      live large brown rat
Business notebook (MINA)
Bedsheet (LUCY)
Valise (HARKER)
Briefcase (HARKER)
Rosary with large crucifix (HARKER)
3 small framed photos (LUCY)
Papers (HARKER)
Small hand mirror (LUCY)
Crude notebook (RENFIELD)
Birdcage with sparrow (RENFIELD)
Paper (ATTENDANT)
Large dead fly (RENFIELD)
Sparrow feather (RENFIELD)
Leather doctor's bag (SEWARD) with:
      small pointed tool
      small glass container
      small jar of ointment
Small white cloth (MINA)
Small bag (MINA)
Leather bound journal (MINA)
Letter (VAN HELSING)
Scarf (LUCY)
Small bottle of liquid (VAN HELSING)
Powder (VAN HELSING)
Drinking glass (VAN HELSING)

Equipment for drawing blood (VAN HELSING)
Cloth (VAN HELSING)
Alcohol (VAN HELSING)
Transfusion devise, with tube and small pump
        (VAN HELSING)
Travel bag (MINA) with:
        journal wrapped with blue ribbon
Hunting knife in sheath (HARKER)
Covered silver platter (DRACULA) with:
        roast chicken
        vegetables
        sliced fruit
Wine bottle, dusty (DRACULA)
Wine glass (DRACULA)
Pitcher (DRACULA)
Basin of water (DRACULA)
Towel (DRACULA)
Mug of shaving cream (HARKER)
Straight razor (HARKER)
Small mirror (HARKER)
Deed (DRACULA)
Writing instrument (DRACULA)
Small cloth sack (DRACULA) with:
        crying baby
Raven (MINA)

ACT TWO

Garlic strings
Large box wrapped with colorful ribbon (MINA) with:
        wreath of garlic
Small, curved sword (RENFIELD)
Tray with teapot and teacup (FEMALE ATTENDANT)
Small hand broom (FEMALE ATTENDANT)
Large, steaming cup of liquid (ATTENDANT)
Rat, bloody (DRACULA)
Newspaper (MINA)

Rosary with large crucifix (MINA)
Lantern (VAN HELSING)
Large cloth bag (HARKER) with:
   large wooden stake
   large hammer
Flat case with white, holy communion wafers
   (VAN HELSING)
Bible (HARKER)
Small hand mirror (SEWARD)
Large wishbone (RENFIELD)
Scarf (MINA)
Wild red roses (VAN HELSING, MINA)
Valise (VAN HELSING)
Large crucifix (VAN HELSING)
Violin (RENFIELD)
Pencil (SEWARD)
Grey ash (SEWARD)

SOUND EFFECTS

Clock ticking
Bell tolling (faint)
Trees rustling
Crashing waves (faint)
Wolves howling (faint)
Crash of thunder
Bats shrieking
Doors slamming shut
Storm
Wolf howl
Thunder
Bats flying
High pitched ringing
Church bells
High pitch ring of glassware
Clock chiming midnight
Piercing howl of wolf
Cock crow
Large doors slamming shut
Soft digging
Many doors being slammed shut and bolted
Passionate breathing
Hissing
Sinister whispers
Heart pounding
Boys choir singing hymns
Mournful tolling of bell
Whip striking flesh
Hissing and rattling of snakes
Child's scream
Loud rustle of branches
Burning, sizzling (quick)
High pitched sound
Large tree snapping in two
Glass breaking
Soft, tolling bell

REAR PROJECTION SURFACE
STOCK STAR DROP
STOCK BLACK SCRIM

BLACK VELOUR LEG

STONE FLOOR
TILE FLOOR

TILE FLOOR
CONCRETE FLOOR

FLAT

DRACULA'S WOODEN BOX

FENCE RUNWAY

PHOENIX FIRE CURTAIN

RAISED UP

TRANSYLVANIA TRIANGLE

FENCE

ACT 2 WINDOW

LUCY'S CHANDELIER

ACT 1 BED

ACT 1 BED

ELEVATOR

LUCY'S WINDOW

FENCE RUNWAY

BIG DRAPE

CHEST

DESK

BENCH

SCENE DESIGN
"DRACULA"

(DESIGNED BY BILL FORRESTER FOR ARIZONA THEATRE COMPANY)

NEW PLAYS

• **SMASH by Jeffrey Hatcher.** Based on the novel, AN UNSOCIAL SOCIALIST by George Bernard Shaw, the story centers on a millionaire Socialist who leaves his bride on their wedding day because he fears his passion for her will get in the way of his plans to overthrow the British government. *"SMASH is witty, cunning, intelligent, and skillful."* –Seattle Weekly. *"SMASH is a wonderfully high-style British comedy of manners that evokes the world of Shaw's high-minded heroes and heroines, but shaped by a post modern sensibility."* –Seattle Herald. [5M, 5W] ISBN: 0-8222-1553-5

• **PRIVATE EYES by Steven Dietz.** A comedy of suspicion in which nothing is ever quite what it seems. *"Steven Dietz's ... Pirandellian smooch to the mercurial nature of theatrical illusion and romantic truth, Dietz's spiraling structure and breathless pacing provide enough of an oxygen rush to revive any moribund audience member ... Dietz's mastery of playmaking ... is cause for kudos."* –The Village Voice. *"The cleverest and most artful piece presented at the 21st annual [Humana] festival was PRIVATE EYES by writer-director Steven Dietz."* –The Chicago Tribune. [3M, 2W] ISBN: 0-8222-1619-1

• **DIMLY PERCEIVED THREATS TO THE SYSTEM by Jon Klein.** Reality and fantasy overlap with hilarious results as this unforgettable family attempts to survive the nineties. *"Here's a play whose point about fractured families goes to the heart, mind -- and ears."* –The Washington Post. *" ... an end-of-the millennium comedy about a family on the verge of a nervous breakdown ... Trenchant and hilarious ... "* –The Baltimore Sun. [2M, 4W] ISBN: 0-8222-1677-9

• **HONOUR by Joanna Murray-Smith.** In a series of intense confrontations, a wife, husband, lover and daughter negotiate the forces of passion, lust, history, responsibility and honour. *"Tight, crackling dialogue (usually played out in punchy verbal duels) captures characters unable to deal with emotions ... Murray-Smith effectively places her characters in situations that strip away pretense."* –Variety. *"HONOUR might just capture a few honors of its own."* –Time Out Magazine. [1M, 3W] ISBN: 0-8222-1683-3

• **NINE ARMENIANS by Leslie Ayvazian.** A revealing portrait of three generations of an Armenian-American family. *" ... Ayvazian's obvious personal exploration ... is evocative, and her picture of an American Life colored nostalgically by an increasingly alien ethnic tradition, is persuasively embedded into a script of a certain supple grace ... "* –The NY Post. *"... NINE ARMENIANS is a warm, likable work that benefits from ... Ayvazian's clear-headed insight into the dynamics of a close-knit family ... "* –Variety. [5M, 5W] ISBN: 0-8222-1602-7

• **PSYCHOPATHIA SEXUALIS by John Patrick Shanley.** Fetishes and psychiatry abound in this scathing comedy about a man and his father's argyle socks. *"John Patrick Shanley's new play, PSYCHOPATHIA SEXUALIS is ... perfectly poised between daffy comedy and believable human neurosis which Shanley combines so well ... "* –The LA Times. *"John Patrick Shanley's PSYCHOPATHIA SEXUALIS is a salty boulevard comedy with a bittersweet theme ... "* –New York Magazine. *"A tour de force of witty, barbed dialogue."* –Variety. [3M, 2W] ISBN: 0-8222-1615-9

DRAMATISTS PLAY SERVICE, INC.
440 Park Avenue South, New York, NY 10016 212-683-8960 Fax 212-213-1539
postmaster@dramatists.com www.dramatists.com

NEW PLAYS

• **A QUESTION OF MERCY by David Rabe.** The Obie Award-winning playwright probes the sensitive and controversial issue of doctor-assisted suicide in the age of AIDS in this poignant drama. *"There are many devastating ironies in Mr. Rabe's beautifully considered, piercingly clear-eyed work ... " –The NY Times. "With unsettling candor and disturbing insight, the play arouses pity and understanding of a troubling subject ... Rabe's provocative tale is an affirmation of dignity that rings clear and true." –Variety.* [6M, 1W] ISBN: 0-8222-1643-4

• **A DOLL'S HOUSE by Henrik Ibsen, adapted by Frank McGuinness. Winner of the 1997 Tony Award for best revival.** *"New, raw, gut-twisting and gripping. Easily the hottest drama this season." –USA Today. "Bold, brilliant and alive." –The Wall Street Journal. "A thunderclap of an evening that takes your breath away." –Time. "The stuff of Broadway legend." –Associated Press.* [4M, 4W, 2 boys] ISBN: 0-8222-1636-1

• **THE WAITING ROOM by Lisa Loomer.** Three women from different centuries meet in a doctor's waiting room in this dark comedy about the timeless quest for beauty -- and its cost. *" ... THE WAITING ROOM ... is a bold, risky melange of conflicting elements that is ... terrifically moving ... There's no resisting the fierce emotional pull of the play." – The NY Times. " ... one of the high points of this year's Off-Broadway season ... THE WAITING ROOM is well worth a visit." –Back Stage.* [7M, 4W, flexible casting] ISBN: 0-8222-1594-2

• **MR. PETERS' CONNECTIONS by Arthur Miller.** Mr. Miller describes the protagonist as existing in a dream-like state when the mind is "freed to roam from real memories to conjectures, from trivialities to tragic insights, from terror of death to glorying in one's being alive." With this memory play, the Tony Award and Pulitzer Prize-winner reaffirms his stature as the world's foremost dramatist. *" ... a cross between Joycean stream-of-consciousness and Strindberg's dream plays, sweetened with a dose of William Saroyan's philosophical whimsy ... CONNECTIONS is most intriguing ... Miller scholars will surely find many connections of their own to make between this work and the author's earlier plays." –The NY Times.* [5M, 3W] ISBN: 0-8222-1687-6

• **THE STEWARD OF CHRISTENDOM by Sebastian Barry.** A freely imagined portrait of the author's great-grandfather, the last Chief Superintendent of the Dublin Metropolitan Police. *"MAGNIFICENT ... the cool, elegiac eye of James Joyce's THE DEAD; the bleak absurdity of Samuel Beckett's lost, primal characters; the cosmic anger of KING LEAR ..." –The NY Times. "Sebastian Barry's compassionate imaging of an ancestor he never knew is among the most poignant onstage displays of humanity in recent memory." –Variety.* [5M, 4W] ISBN: 0-8222-1609-4

• **SYMPATHETIC MAGIC by Lanford Wilson. Winner of the 1997 Obie for best play.** The mysteries of the universe, and of human and artistic creation, are explored in this award-winning play. *"Lanford Wilson's idiosyncratic SYMPATHETIC MAGIC is his BEST PLAY YET ... the rare play you WANT ... chock-full of ideas, incidents, witty or poetic lines, scientific and philosophical argument ... you'll find your intellectual faculties racing." – New York Magazine. "The script is like a fully notated score, next to which most new plays are cursory lead sheets." –The Village Voice.* [5M, 3W] ISBN: 0-8222-1630-2

DRAMATISTS PLAY SERVICE, INC.
440 Park Avenue South, New York, NY 10016 212-683-8960 Fax 212-213-1539
postmaster@dramatists.com www.dramatists.com